PREFACE

This report contains information on the nutritional requirements, signs of deficiencies, growth rates, feed and water requirements, and toxic levels of certain elements for poultry. The references at the end of the report can be consulted for additional details.

The material contained herein should be useful to all who are concerned with formulation and manufacturing of poultry diets and for students and teachers of poultry nutrition. Owners of feed mills, high-school teachers, county agricultural agents, and poultry hobbyists will also find the information helpful.

The requirements are intended to serve as a basis for formulation of the various poultry rations. The scope of these requirements has been expanded as interest in other species of poultry has increased and as information has become available.

This seventh revised edition of *Nutrient Requirements of Poultry* has been developed and built upon foundations laid down in previous editions. The contributions of the authors of the previous revisions are recognized in developing this report. The first report, entitled *Recommended Nutrient Allowances for Poultry*, was published in June 1944 and initiated an extensive series of publications from the National Academy of Sciences, "Nutrient Requirements of Domestic Animals." The same title was used for editions published in 1946 and 1950. In 1954, the title was changed to *Nutrient Requirements for Poultry*. This title was modified to its present form in 1960, reprinted in 1962 with minor revisions, and revised in 1966 and 1971. Early reports under the title included *only* chickens and turkeys. In 1954, ducks were added, and in 1960, pheasants and quail. Geese are included in this revision.

Because of many requests for standard reference diets, the subcommittee decided to include two diets in this report that should give satisfactory growth under laboratory conditions. These diets could serve as a reference control in several types of experiments with growing chickens.

The subcommittee is indebted to Philip Ross, Executive Secretary, and Selma P. Baron, Staff Assistant, of the Board on Agriculture and Renewable Resources for their assistance in the production of this report; to the members of the Committee on Animal Nutrition for their suggestions; to C. W. Carlson, D. R. Clandinin, L. W. Luther, D. F. Middendorf, and A. R. Robblee for their comprehensive reviews and constructive comments on the report; and to William P. Flatt, Director, Agricultural Experiment Stations, University of Georgia, who served as liaison between the Committee on Animal Nutrition and the Board on Agriculture and Renewable Resources.

The subcommittee also wishes to express its thanks to scientists in industry and in various laboratories for providing some of the information on feedstuff composition and on growth rates of the various species.

Subcommittee on Poultry Nutrition

Milton L. Sunde, *Chairman*
James R. Couch
Leo S. Jensen
Beryl E. March
Edward C. Naber
Lawrence M. Potter
Paul E. Waibel

Committee on Animal Nutrition

Robert R. Oltjen, *Chairman*
Clarence B. Ammerman
John P. Bowland
Charles W. Deyoe
Joseph P. Fontenot
Edward C. Naber
Gary L. Rumsey
Loris H. Schultz
Richard G. Warner

v

CONTENTS

INTRODUCTION

In establishing values for the requirements of poultry for the various nutrients, the subcommittee has reviewed and evaluated published results of nutritional research. In addition, specialists in related areas have been consulted. Some calculations and interpolations have been necessary because of gaps in knowledge in scientific reports. In formulation of diets and for completing specifications for computer programming, it is necessary to use figures for *all* involved nutrients.

Where the requirements are well delineated, the "established requirement" is indicated in the tables by regular type. When the information available to the subcommittee was sparse or when published results did not agree, the numerals in the tables are in lightface type and the term "estimated requirement" is used.

The values reported, whether "established" or "estimated," were not increased by a "margin of safety." They represent the judgment of the subcommittee after reviewing the published data. The criteria of adequacy included growth, health, reproduction, feed efficiency, and quality of animal products.

Unfortunately, in many instances, definitive data are not available for a statement of an exact nutrient requirement. In some of these situations extrapolations or interpolations have been made and estimated requirements thus derived. In some situations, the subcommittee preferred to leave the column blank or insert a question mark.

Frequently, temperature or other environmental factors is not specified in the reports presenting requirement data. Fortunately, most experiments have been conducted in environments acceptable to the caretakers themselves. Therefore, these average conditions will approximate those encountered by poultry in normal housing. When temperature or humidity conditions deviate much from 16°–21°C (60°–75°F) and 40–60 percent relative humidity, adjustments in nutrient levels should be made to compensate for changes in feed intake. Data are being accumulated that will provide information on nutrient needs under higher and lower temperature conditions.

It is recognized that there are genetic differences among strains that affect nutrient requirements. In this report, consideration has been given to differences in requirements between broiler-type and egg-type strains of chickens.

The nutrient composition of feedstuffs is variable. Inadequate feed mixing, improper processing, and unfavorable storage conditions may reduce effective levels of nutrients. The nutritionist may accordingly add a "margin of safety" to the stated requirements in arriving at nutrient allowances to be used in formulation in order to compensate for the above-mentioned conditions. The requirements are stated with the assumption of 88 percent dry matter in the ration. This will closely approximate most feeding conditions.

Detailed information on dietary-restricted food intake is also appearing in the scientific literature. The complexity of this consideration, however, does not yet permit its discussion here except in general terms.

1

NUTRIENT REQUIREMENTS

The feedstuffs used in poultry feeds provide several classes of nutrients. These will be considered briefly in this section, and signs of deficiencies will be discussed in greater detail in the subsequent sections. The actual requirement values selected by the subcommittee for the individual nutrients are given in Tables 1 through 8. The values are expressed in percentages or in amounts per kilogram of feed. In some tables, it has been possible to report values in grams of amino acid per megacalorie (g/Mcal) because there has been sufficient work reported to justify this inclusion. In subsequent tables, the requirements per day have been compiled and calculated based on "normal" feed consumption. In actual formulation, these figures will almost always have to be converted to units per unit weight of feed because the birds are generally fed in groups on an *ad libitum* basis.

ENERGY

Terminology and Determination

There are several ways that the energy value of a feed ingredient for poultry rations can be expressed. Energy terms for feedstuffs have been defined and discussed in detail in *Biological Energy Interrelationships and Glossary of Energy Terms* (NAS-NRC publication 1411). Because many individuals may not have ready access to the detailed report, a brief description of some of the terms used in poultry feeding appears below.

Calorie (cal) is the heat required to raise the temperature of 1 g of water from 14.5°C to 15.5°C. However, since the specific heat of water changes with temperature, a calorie may be defined more precisely as 4.1860 international joules.

Kilocalorie (kcal) is 1,000 calories and is the usual unit of energy used by the North American poultry feed industry.

Megacalorie (Mcal) is 1,000,000 calories and is commonly used as the basis for expressing requirements for other nutrients.

Gross Energy (GE) is the amount of heat, measured in calories, that is released when a substance is completely oxidized in a bomb calorimeter under 25 to 30 atmospheres of oxygen.

Apparent Digestible Energy (DE) is the gross energy of the feed consumed minus gross energy of the feces.

DE = (GE of food per unit dry wt × dry wt of food) −
(GE of feces per unit dry wt × dry wt of feces)

Avian species excrete feces and urine via a common cloaca, thus making it difficult to measure digestibility. Consequently, DE values are of no practical interest in poultry feed formulation.

Apparent Metabolizable Energy (ME) is the food intake gross energy minus fecal energy, minus energy in the gaseous products of digestion, minus urinary energy. For birds, the gaseous products are usually negligible, so that ME is the food intake gross energy minus the excreta gross energy. A correction for nitrogen retained in the body is frequently applied to yield an ME_n value. This is the most common measure of available energy in poultry nutrition.

True Metabolizable Energy (TME) for birds is the food intake gross energy minus the excretal energy of food origin. A correction for nitrogen retention may be applied to yield a TME_n value. Most energy values in the literature have been determined in assays in which the test material is substituted for part of the test diet or for some ingredient of known ME value. When the birds in these assays are fed *ad libitum* the values obtained, although apparent ME values, approximate TME values for most feedstuffs, being only slightly lower.

Net Energy (NE) is the difference between metabolizable energy and the heat increment and includes the amount of energy used for maintenance only (NE_m) or for maintenance plus production (NE_{m+p}). Productive energy, once a popular measure of energy available to poultry, is an estimation of net energy.

The energy values of feedstuffs presented in the tables are expressed both as kilocalories of metabolizable energy and productive energy per kilogram. The productive energy values are estimates of net energy as determined by Fraps (1946) and modified by Titus (1961) and others, based on a comparative slaughter technique. The metabolizable energy values are summarized from data published by several investigators who used the methods developed by Hill and Anderson (1958) for determining ME of feedstuffs for poultry.

Productive energy values were once commonly used by feed manufacturers for calculating the energy value of poultry feeds, but most now use ME values. Although the latter values are readily determined and reproducible, there is evidence that they do not accurately describe the potential of the energy in a diet to promote growth or egg production. For growth and fattening of poultry, ME contributed by lipids is utilized more efficiently than that contributed by carbohydrates, and ME of proteins is utilized less efficiently than that of carbohydrates.

Research on improved ways to express the utilizable energy in feedstuffs has continued. DeGroote (1974) proposed values of 75, 90, and 60 percent, respectively, for the net ME utilization of available carbohydrates (sugars and starches), fat, and proteins in poultry feedstuffs. He developed calculated net energy values for feedstuffs by multiplying the ME value by an average efficiency of utilization, which was determined by adding the products of the relative percentages of crude protein, crude fat, and available carbohydrate in the ingredient with their respective utilization coefficients of 60, 90, and 75 percent. Although the DeGroote net energy system theoretically should be a somewhat more accurate assessment of the useful energy in feedstuffs for poultry, it has received limited use by both research investigators and feed manufacturers.

A new method for estimating TME values of feedstuffs for poultry has also been proposed by Sibbald (1976). These TME values are higher than ME values, but they have the apparent advantage of being unaffected by variations in feed intake. Further experimentation is necessary to determine if these values for feedstuffs would have advantages over the presently used ME values.

The figure below was derived by taking gross energy figures for a diet composed of 750 g of corn, 50 g of nonenergy components, and 200 g of soybean meal per

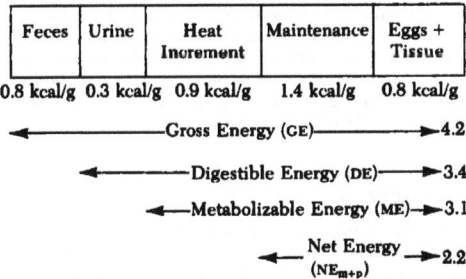

kilo (kg) and calculating the gross, the metabolizable, and the net or productive energy of this diet. The diagram illustrates the losses of energy at various stages after ingestion of 1 g of the above diet by a hen and shows the quantitative relationship of the energy terms.

In general, a corn-soy mixture will have about 4,000 kcal of gross energy/kg of feed, about 3,000 metabolizable kcal/kg of feed, and about 2,000 net or productive energy kcal/kg of feed. Both metabolizable and productive energies can vary due to the composition of the feedstuffs, but other factors (e.g., age, species, genetics, and strain of the bird and the environment) also may have an influence. Virtually all metabolizable energy values of feedstuffs have been determined with young chicks; data are needed for different ages of chickens and turkeys.

Requirements

Birds tend to eat to satisfy their energy requirements if fed free choice. Consequently, it is possible, within limits, to regulate the intake of all nutrients, except water, by including them in the diet in specific ratios to available energy. Thus, the energy content of the diet must be considered in formulating to meet a desired intake of all essential nutrients other than energy itself.

It is impossible to set an energy requirement in terms of kilocalories per kilogram of diet (kcal/kg) because birds adjust their feed intake to obtain the necessary daily requirement of energy. Further, temperature of the environment has a large influence on feed intake. The warmer the environment, the less the feed intake; therefore, the requirement for all nutrients, expressed as a percent of the diet, is dependent upon the environmental temperature. Other variables are: health, genetics, form of feed, nutritional balance, stress, body size, and rate of egg production or growth.

It is believed that feed intake is, in part, controlled by the amount of glucose in the blood. It has been observed that the addition of fat to the diet results in overconsumption on the part of the bird. As a result, some variation in the protein:energy ratio may be tolerated. In general, when dietary protein levels are low in relation to energy and with *ad libitum* feeding, fat deposition is markedly increased; with higher levels of protein, less fat is deposited. Increasing the protein level above that required for maximum growth rate reduces fat deposition still further.

To establish the nutrient requirements of poultry, some assumptions must be made. It is assumed that the environmental temperature in which poultry of various species and age are grown is ideal or as near optimum as known at present for efficient production of growth and reproduction. Therefore, the energy level of the diet was first established for each species and age of poultry, and then the other nutrients were determined based upon the established level of energy. If a higher level of energy is used in the diet, feed consumption will decrease and the minimum level of other nutrients should be increased in

Feces	Urine	Heat Increment	Maintenance	Eggs + Tissue
0.8 kcal/g	0.3 kcal/g	0.9 kcal/g	1.4 kcal/g	0.8 kcal/g

◄——————Gross Energy (GE)——————►4.2

◄——————Digestible Energy (DE)——————►3.4

◄——Metabolizable Energy (ME)—►3.1

◄—— Net Energy (NE$_{m+p}$) ——►2.2

proportion to the energy content. Similarly, if a lower dietary energy level is used, then proportionately lower levels of other nutrients should be used in the diet.

Birds are often subjected to a restricted or a controlled feed intake level that anticipates daily energy requirements for desired growth rate or more efficient egg production. In such instances, *ad libitum* consumption of the diet would result in overconsumption of energy.

The energy requirement may be defined as that amount of available energy that will provide for growth or egg production at a high enough level to permit maximal economic return for the production unit.

An animal, through its genetic makeup and environmental circumstances, has a certain potential for performance. The level of dietary energy (and associated nutritional balance) in the prescribed diet should be high enough to allow expression of this potential, within economic limitations.

If a broiler is fed a diet that is high in oats, there may be an energy deficiency. If a turkey breeder hen is fed a similar diet, energy may be adequate. The difference is that the broiler is unable to consume enough of the diet to produce at its maximum rate, while the turkey breeder hen can do so. Birds may expend more energy eating bulkier feeds and, therefore, have less energy available for growth and fattening but usually enough for egg production. Pelleting of a bulky diet would help the broiler to eat enough of the medium-energy diet and reduce the amount of energy expended for eating. Adding fat makes it possible for the broiler to consume more energy at the same feed intake.

The use of a mechanical extruder to process soybean meal or corn can result in expanding the product so that the growing bird cannot eat enough to permit maximum gains. Pelleting this type of product will reduce the volume and restore the growth rate to normal.

In view of the foregoing, under *ad libitum* feeding conditions, the nutritionist must select a dietary energy level that will allow sufficient consumption of the balanced diet to provide the opportunity for maximum economic return. The following generalizations will aid in achieving this objective under average conditions. It should be borne in mind that, if the diet is pelleted, maximum growth or egg production may be achieved with somewhat lower dietary ME. Milo or wheat may be considered equivalent to corn in the corn-soy diets.

Chicken Broilers For the starting and finishing periods, corn-, milo-, or wheat-soybean diets containing 0–10 percent fat are appropriate. Lower-energy diets are not normally used.

Chickens for Egg Production During the starting period, corn-, milo-, or wheat-soybean diets are appropriate. For the growing period, the same would be true although there may be an inclination to use a lower-energy diet. The same type diets with a range of 0–3 percent fat or 0–25 percent oats or barley are satisfactory for layers under floor management. With layers in cages, a fat level of 0–2 percent fat or 0–25 percent oats or barley is satisfactory. For layers in cages, the maximum energy level may be somewhat lower because of limited exercise, which may result in obesity and/or fatty liver.

Breeders for Meat Production During the growing period, the energy intake should be lower than recommended for broiler chickens or turkeys. This can be accomplished through physical restriction of the diet or lighting or a combination thereof. During the breeding period, it is also appropriate to use a lower-energy diet or restrict intake of the diet to prevent the development of obesity in the birds.

Turkeys For starting and growing turkeys, diets containing as high an energy level as the higher protein level will permit should be fed. For holding and breeding turkeys, with corn-, milo-, or wheat-soybean diets, a lower-energy concentration would be appropriate.

Energy Values in Tables

The ME values in the requirement tables are not intended as *requirements*. They are provided to give perspective to the other nutrient requirement levels. Using the energy level for reference will enable the nutritionist to form a ratio of the amount of nutrient per unit of energy, thereby keeping the nutrients in balance with available energy. In eating to satisfy its energy need, an animal will eat less of a high-energy diet and more of a low-energy diet. Having the nutrients in relation to dietary energy will ensure proper intake on a daily basis.

The table opposite shows the effects of adding high-fiber, low-calorie feedstuffs to a typical corn-soy diet and the effects of increasing the energy level by incorporating 5–10 percent added fat into the diet and illustrates the potential range of energy levels used in practical diets for poultry of various ages. For instance, adding 40 percent oat hulls to a growing diet for egg-strain pullets will reduce the energy to 1,860 from 3,150 kcal.

PROTEIN AND AMINO ACIDS

Requirements

Where sufficient information is available on amino acid requirements, protein nutrition can be considered solely on the basis of constituent amino acids. Protein levels are listed primarily as an aid in describing diets in the field and because most feed-control regulations require a statement of minimum protein.

DAILY FEED CONSUMPTION MUST BE CONSIDERED

The importance of feed consumption and its relationship to temperature have been discussed in the energy section. The energy influence on feed consumption is cer-

Species, Period (Weeks of Age)	40% Oat Hulls	25% Oats 15% Middlings 10% Bran	10% Oats 10% Middlings	Corn-Soy	Added Fat 5%	10%
	Δ − 1,100ᵃ	− 550	− 200	0	+ 200	+ 400
Turkeys				(kcal/kg)		
♂0–4 ♀0–4				2,840		
4–8 4–8				2,910		
8–12 8–11				2,990		
12–16 11–14				3,080		
16–20 14–17				3,160		
20–Fᵇ 17–Fᵇ				3,235		
22–30 Prebreeding				3,200		
30–60 Breeding				2,900		
Chicken—Broiler						
0–3 Starting				3,000		
3–5 Growing				3,100		
5– Withdrawal				3,200		
Chicken—Egg Type						
0–8 Starting				3,000		
8–20 Growing (1,860)				3,150		
20–80 Laying—floor				2,850		
Laying—cage				2,850		
Chicken—Meat-Type Breeders						
0–8 Starting				3,000		
8–20 Growingᶜ				3,150		
20–70 Breedingᶜ				2,850		

ᵃKilocalories of ME/kilogram.
ᵇF = Finish.
ᶜUse controlled feeding of corn-soy diet.
Δ = Approximate change in ME per kilogram with diet modification shown.
NOTE: Solid line represents typical diet type; broken line represents acceptable diet type.

tainly the major factor to be considered at moderate temperatures. A slightly low protein intake, however, can raise feed consumption. These relationships have increased interest in other ways to express protein and amino acid needs, rather than as a percent of the diet.

Considerably more research is needed in the general area of amino acid requirements. As presented, the requirement has no reference to environmental conditions, e.g., ambient temperature. In regard to the latter, it may generally be assumed that the listed requirements are for a moderate climate (16°–24°C [60°–75°F]). It is believed that the percentage requirements should be raised or lowered in warmer or colder environments, respectively, in accordance with expected differences in feed or energy intake, so that a certain daily intake of the amino acid is assured. The amino acid levels presented should allow maximum or near-maximum growth and production. In a period of relatively high protein prices, the levels may be reduced slightly, lowering growth somewhat, but thereby achieving a saving of protein and possibly greater economic return.

For the first time in this NRC publication, amino acid requirements of growing chickens are stated on a "per megacalorie" basis as well as percent of the diet (note Tables 1 and 2). In this instance the term is grams of amino acid per megacalorie (ME). It is sometimes more convenient to use percent per megacalorie, i.e., 1.44 percent = 4.5 g/Mcal = 0.45 percent Mcal. The conversions to the percentage method are as follows: if energy is listed per kilogram of diet, merely move the decimal of the values one place to the left; if energy is listed per pound of diet, move the decimal one place to the left and multiply by 2.2046.

Amino acid requirements for laying hens (Table 2) are presented in relation to dietary metabolizable energy and on a daily intake basis. The latter provides a means of adjusting to varying feed intake, especially as modified by ambient temperature or dietary energy concentration. In using the daily amino acid intake concept, it is desirable to measure actual flock feed intake.

Requirements for amino acids of turkeys, ducks, and other species are listed as percent of the diet since the metabolizable energy values used as the basis for the amino acid requirement are specified.

PRODUCTIVE STATE OF THE ANIMAL

It is well recognized that amino acid requirements are positively related to rate of growth or intensity of egg production. For instance, the poult has a high amino acid requirement per day because it is growing rapidly. The adult male chicken has a very low requirement in relation to the laying hen even though body size is actually greater and feed consumption is about the same.

GENETIC CONSTITUTION OF THE BIRD

Even among poultry of similar species, body size, growth rate, or egg production, there may be differences in requirements among strains. It is a research challenge to elucidate these differences.

Nutritional Factors Influence Requirement

PROTEIN LEVEL

Amino acid requirements tend to increase with increased dietary protein. With suboptimal protein levels, adding the most-limiting amino acid increases the growth rate or productivity considerably. Excessive dietary protein also affects energy needs and may alter amino acid requirements. It is normally desirable to meet the requirements of all the amino acids as closely as possible, avoiding excesses of amino acids or protein.

SPECIFIC AMINO ACID RELATIONSHIPS

Methionine-Cystine The requirement for methionine can be met only by methionine, while the requirement for cystine may be met by cystine or methionine. This is because methionine is readily converted to cystine metabolically, while the reverse is not possible. If sulfate is deficient, a portion of the cystine that is normally converted to sulfate metabolically may be spared by the addition of sulfates to the diet (as sodium or potassium sulfate).

Phenylalanine-Tyrosine The requirement for phenylalanine may be met only by phenylalanine, while the requirement for tyrosine may be met by tyrosine or phenylalanine.

Glycine-Serine Glycine and serine can be used interchangeably in poultry diets. Normally, when the overall protein requirement is met, the amount of dietary glycine or serine is also adequate.

ANTAGONISM

There are specific antagonisms among amino acids that may be structurally related, e.g., valine-leucine-isoleucine and arginine-lysine. Increasing one or two of such a group may raise the need for another of the same group. The level of leucine is high when corn gluten meal containing 60 percent protein and corn make up most of the diet.

IMBALANCE

In supplementing diets with limiting amino acids it is important to supplement first with the most-limiting one, followed by the second-most-limiting one. Inadvertent oversupplementation with only the second-most-limiting amino acid may create an imbalance and accentuate the primary deficiency.

CONVERSION OF AMINO ACIDS TO VITAMINS

High levels of methionine may partly compensate for a deficiency of choline or vitamin B_{12} by providing needed methyl groups, and high levels of tryptophan may alleviate a niacin deficiency through metabolic conversion to niacin. However, these conversions are of theoretical interest only, as it would be poor economics to satisfy a vitamin deficiency by addition of relatively more expensive amino acids.

Other Problems in Meeting Amino Acid Requirements

AMINO ACID AVAILABILITY

When diets are calculated based upon feed composition and analysis information, the assumption is usually made that amino acids are 80–90 percent available. This assumption is not necessarily valid. By-products such as feathers or blood are either indigestible in native form or made indigestible by overheating in processing, respectively. In such cases, the product must either be demonstrated to contain highly available amino acids, or availability coefficients should be used as formulation modifiers. Certain other feedstuffs such as meat scraps and soybean meal are also affected by treatment during normal manufacturing processes. As more research is done in this area, it may be possible to reduce our estimates of amino acid requirement levels and use amino acid tables that consider the availability factor. The results of amino acid determinations on the same feedstuff between different laboratories, unfortunately, differ considerably. When this occurs, a small difference in availability (between 80 or 90 percent for a particular amino acid) in a feedstuff becomes relatively unimportant.

VARIATION OF INDIVIDUAL FEEDSTUFFS IN PROTEIN CONTENT AND AMINO ACID LEVELS

This problem causes much concern with ration formulators. Frequently, the particular sample of an ingredient is already on the way to the poultry house before the analysis has been completed.

CONSEQUENCE OF PROTEIN OR AMINO ACID DEFICIENCY

Severe deficiency

- Feed intake stops
- Tongue deformity with leucine, isoleucine, and phenylalanine deficiency
- Egg production stops in 4–5 days
- Body weight loss
- Resorption of ova

• Stasis of digestive tract
• Death

Borderline deficiency

• Poor growth and feathering (see Figure 1)
• Reduced egg size
• Poor egg production (hatchability is not affected)
• Lack of melanin pigment in black- or reddish-colored feathers with low lysine
• Tendency toward greater deposition of carcass and liver fat. When the calorie-protein ratio is too wide, growth rate or egg production diminishes. Accompanying this is a slight overconsumption of feed (an attempt to consume enough protein?), resulting in greater carcass and/or liver fat
Widening the calorie-protein ratio may be used to improve finish of turkey roaster-fryers, but is not a popular practice because growth is depressed
• Poorer efficiency of conversion of feed into eggs or meat

Another problem with some protein feedstuffs is that they may contain toxic compounds. A good example is cottonseed meal, which may contain gossypol. The tolerance for gossypol is greater in older than in younger animals. For growth, poultry are less sensitive than swine, but discoloration of the yolks in stored eggs can occur at levels lower than those that affect swine. Ferrous sulfate additions to furnish about 600 ppm iron prevent yolk discoloration from as much as 150 ppm of gossypol.

The development of cotton cultivars with very low levels of gossypol has considerably increased the use of cottonseed meals in laying rations. Prepress solvent meals contain more gossypol than those processed by the screw press or direct-solvent method.

There are also problems with rapeseed meals and the goitrogenic compounds that certain strains contain in levels high enough to be toxic. Geneticists have been able to develop strains that contain low levels of these materials.

Even soybean meal, the most-used protein supplement, contains harmful substances, such as a trypsin inhibitor, but these are destroyed by proper heating. Heat treatment improves the utilization of the protein in this excellent feedstuff. The urease test is a common chemical method to determine underheating. This generally requires access to a laboratory. A simple on-the-farm test can be used to estimate the amount of heat to which the meal has been subjected. This involves putting 10 level teaspoons of the suspect soybean meal in a jar with an airtight lid. One teaspoon of urea is mixed with the meal, and then 5 teaspoons of water are added and the resulting mixture is stirred again. The lid is then screwed on securely, and the sample is allowed to stand at room temperature for 20 minutes. At that time, the lid should be removed and the jar sniffed for ammonia. If there is an odor of ammonia, the meal has been underheated. All meals will develop ammonia by the next day if the jar is left closed for that period.

MINERALS

Minerals are required for the formation of the skeleton, as parts of hormones or as activators of enzymes, and for the proper maintenance of necessary osmotic relationships within the body of the bird. Calcium and phosphorus are important in the formation and maintenance of the skeletal structures of the body. Sodium, potassium, magnesium, and chloride function with phosphates and bicarbonates to maintain homeostasis, osmotic relationships, and an optimum pH throughout the body. Requirements for these macro elements are listed in Tables 3, 5, 6, and some of them in Tables 7 and 8. Certain trace elements are also listed in the tables.

Most of the calcium in the diet of the growing chicken is used for bone formation, whereas, in the mature laying fowl, most is used in egg-shell formation. Calcium is essential for blood clotting and is required along with sodium and potassium for maintaining normal heart function. An excess of calcium interferes with the utilization of magnesium, manganese, and zinc and may decrease the palatability of the diet.

Phosphorus is required in large amounts for bone formation, but it also has important functions in the metabolism of carbohydrates and fats and is a component of all living cells. This mineral likewise is required for maintenance of the acid-base balance of the body as well as for calcium transport in egg formation. The ratio of phosphorus to calcium is vital, especially for young poultry. Generally, a ratio of about 1:1.2 (P:Ca) is considered to be ideal. Ratios from 1:1 to 1:1.5 are, however, well tolerated. For the laying bird, obviously, the ratio must be wider (1:4 or more).

It is important that the minimum level of available inorganic phosphorus be provided. The stated requirement is based on the generally greater availability of inorganic phosphorus than that of phytin phosphorus.

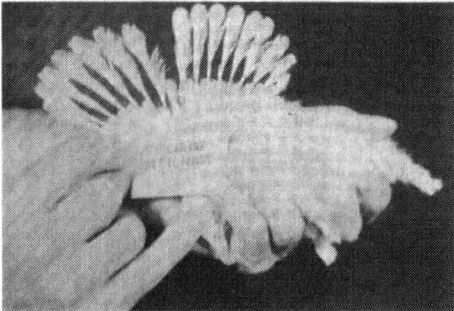

FIGURE 1 Feather abnormality produced by an arginine deficiency. (Courtesy of the University of Wisconsin.)

Approximately 30 percent of the phosphorus in plant products is considered to be available to the young chick, poult, or duckling; the older bird has the ability to use most, if not all, of the phytin or organic phosphorus in plant products. Inorganic phosphorus supplements are listed in Table 21. The biological availability of the phosphorus in these supplements may vary.

The calcium requirement of the laying hen is difficult to define. The requirement has been increased to 3.25 percent, which is believed to be optimum for conditions usually prevailing in moderate climates. Hens that are subjected to a temperature of 33°C (90°F) may require a calcium level of 3.5–3.75 percent. Finely pulverized limestone may adversely affect feed intake when used to provide these higher calcium levels. Growing pullets fed calcium in amounts that are too high or too low are subject to difficulties in calcium metabolism after the onset of egg production. Older hens use calcium less efficiently. The biological availability of calcium is high in most sources used except dolomitic limestone. The latter contains high levels of magnesium.

Sodium or sodium chloride is essential for all animals. Generally, levels that just support maximum gains or productivity are used because higher levels lead to excessive consumption of water and problems with moisture and ventilation in the poultry house. Provided adequate water is available, chickens and turkeys can ingest well over 1.0 percent sodium chloride without decreasing productivity.

As soils become leached, their content of trace minerals and the feedstuffs grown on them become borderline or deficient; it is therefore necessary to add more of certain minerals to poultry diets. Interactions between various trace minerals, such as copper and molybdenum, selenium and mercury, calcium and zinc, or calcium and manganese, are also important considerations in poultry nutrition. Selenium is also metabolically involved with vitamin E and arsenic.

Other Trace Minerals Added to Certain Purified Protein Diets

Often nutritionists and others formulate diets composed of ingredients not ordinarily used in poultry feeds. When this is done, additions of the trace minerals listed below may be desirable, depending on the experimental design. It has been determined that several of these mineral elements are essential under very special conditions. Requirements are not established for these elements, but the following may be taken as guidelines:

Element	mg/kg of Diet
Silicon	250
Vanadium	0.2
Tin	3
Nickel	0.1
Molybdenum	1
Chromium	3

VITAMINS

Vitamins are generally classified under two headings: fat-soluble vitamins A, D, E, and K; and water-soluble vitamins, which include so-called B-complex vitamins and vitamin C (ascorbic acid). Vitamin C is synthesized by poultry and is, accordingly, not considered as a required dietary nutrient. There is some evidence, nevertheless, of a favorable response to vitamin C by birds under the stress of high temperature.

The requirements for most vitamins are given in terms of milligrams per kilogram of diet. Exceptions are vitamins A, D, and E, for which the requirements are commonly given in units. Units are used to express the requirements for these vitamins because different forms of these vitamins have quite different biological activities.

For example, requirements for vitamin A are expressed in either International Units (IU) or United States Pharmacopeia units (USP) per kilogram of diet. The international standards for vitamin A activity based on vitamin A and β-carotene are as follows:

1 IU of vitamin A = 1 USP unit = vitamin A activity of 0.3 μg of crystalline vitamin A alcohol (retinol) or 0.344 μg of vitamin A acetate or 0.550 μg of vitamin A palmitate. β-Carotene is the standard for provitamin A. One IU of vitamin A activity is equivalent to the activity of 0.6 μg of β-carotene, i.e., 1 mg of β-carotene = 1,667 IU of vitamin A.

Requirements for vitamin D are expressed in International Chick Units (ICU), which are based on the activity of vitamin D_3. Birds use vitamin D_3 from fish oils and irradiated animal sterol effectively, but they do not use vitamin D_2 from irradiated plant sterol as effectively as do rats and other mammals. One ICU of vitamin D is defined as the vitamin D activity of 0.025 μg of vitamin D_3 (cholecalciferol). The potency of an unknown sample, if it is to be expressed in ICU, must be measured with chicks rather than with rats because of the different responses of the two species to vitamin D_2. The listed requirements for vitamin D are based on the recommendations for minimum quantities of inorganic phosphorus and calcium to be supplied in the diet.

One IU of vitamin E is the activity of 1 mg of synthetic DL-α-tocopheryl acetate. One milligram each of D-α-tocopheryl acetate, D-α-tocopherol, and DL-α-tocopherol have activities of 1.36, 1.49, and 1.1 IUs, respectively. The dietary requirement for vitamin E is highly variable and depends upon the level and type of fat in the diet, the level of selenium, and the presence of antioxidants other than vitamin E.

Several compounds with vitamin K activity are known. The naturally occurring forms are K_1 phylloquinone (2-methyl-3-phytyl-1,4-naphthoquinone) and K_2 menaquinone (as basic K_1 plus two to seven isoprene units). A synthetic fat-soluble compound, menadione (2-methyl-1,4-naphthoquinone), and three water-soluble compounds, menadione sodium bisulfite (MSB), menadione sodium bisulfite complex (MSBC), and menadione dimethylpyrimidol bisulfite (MPB), are also active.

If menadione is considered as a reference material, the MSB has, theoretically, a menadione content of 66 percent, the MPB 45.5 percent, and the MSBC 32.8 percent. On an equal molar basis, the relative theoretical potency of MPB to MSBC would be 1.39. The activity of the various synthetic compounds depends on the stability of the preparations developed for use by the feed industry. When sulfaquinoxaline is used to increase prothrombin time, the naturally occurring forms are more effective in counteracting this action than is menadione. Additional experiments should be conducted to determine the relative effectiveness of the commercial products available.

The requirements for the water-soluble vitamins may, in some cases, be provided by the amounts occurring naturally in the customary feedstuffs used in compounding rations. As shortages of the conventional feedstuffs become more common, however, the products used in substitution may not supply sufficient amounts of various vitamins. Formulators of poultry feeds should therefore be alert to the need for supplementation with vitamins hitherto assumed to be amply distributed in the feedstuffs.

The requirements for the water-soluble vitamins are interrelated and also dependent upon the nature of the diet. The type of carbohydrate, protein level, and amino acid balance are major factors determining the dietary requirement for several vitamins. Betaine is widely distributed in practical feedstuffs and may be important in sparing choline. The growing chicken can use betaine interchangeably with choline to meet its needs for methylating agents, but betaine cannot replace choline in preventing perosis. Likewise, vitamin B_{12} has been shown to reduce the requirement for choline. The choline requirements given in the tables are applicable to diets that contain the specified amounts of vitamin B_{12}.

XANTHOPHYLLS

Xanthophylls are useful in poultry diets to provide yellow coloration in egg yolks and the yellow skin color in broiler and roaster carcasses. Frequently, processors of egg yolks are interested in producing dark-colored yolks to maximize coloration in egg noodles and other food products. About 60 mg of xanthophyll per kg of diet is needed to produce a very dark-colored yolk.

Only a few natural products contain significant quantities of xanthophyll. Yellow corn and alfalfa products lose xanthophyll or lutein relatively quickly. For instance, corn stored for a year loses a considerable part of its lutein. Extremely high levels of vitamin A will also reduce the yellow color in yolks. Dietary ethoxyquin will increase yolk pigmentation slightly. The xanthophylls in algae and marigold are utilized less efficiently than those in corn and alfalfa.

The following table shows the xanthophyll content of a few feedstuffs.

Feedstuff	Xanthophyll, mg/kg
Alfalfa meal, 17% protein	200
Alfalfa meal, 20% protein	240
Alfalfa meal, 25% protein	480
Alfalfa juice protein, 40% protein	800
Algae, common, dried	2,000
Corn, yellow	22
Corn gluten meal, 41% protein	132
Corn gluten meal, 60% protein	350
Marigold petal meal	7,000

The coloration of the shanks and skin is reduced when coccidiosis and certain other diseases are present.

UNIDENTIFIED NUTRIENTS

Many reports published during the past three decades provide evidence for the existence of unidentified factors that stimulate growth, increase reproduction, improve product quality, or reduce toxicity of mineral elements in poultry. Unidentified factors have been reported in egg yolk, whey, yeast, marine-fish and packing-house by-products, soybeans, distillers' solubles, corn, green forages, fermentation residues, and other natural materials. Some of the biological responses observed from crude materials in earlier reports have been shown subsequently to be due to zinc or other known nutrients. Several trace elements recently shown to be essential for animals may have been involved in some of the responses.

Some materials, particularly marine-fish products, have usually stimulated growth or reproduction on a wide variety of basal diets well fortified with all the known nutrients. Some evidence exists that the factor found in marine-fish products is a low-molecular-weight organic substance that can be liberated or extracted by several organic solvents and that can be transmitted through the egg from the breeder hen to her offspring. Evidence has been obtained that phenolic acids may explain part of the growth responses obtained with distillers' solubles. Growth of Japanese quail fed a diet composed of amino acids is increased when intact protein is included in the diet, suggesting that certain peptides are required for maximum growth. Interpretation of growth-stimulating effects from crude materials is complicated by possible changes in the gastrointestinal populations of microorganisms. Growth responses to crude materials have tended to be greater when large responses were obtained from antibiotic supplementation.

Feeding of purified diets to breeding chickens, turkeys, and Japanese quail results in lower egg production and hatchability of fertile eggs than that obtained with practical diets. Adding crude materials such as fish solubles, alfalfa meal, and distillers' dried grains with solubles to the purified diets usually increases egg production and hatchability. Adding high levels of dried corn steep liquor concentrate, brewers' dried grains, or distillers' dried grains with solubles to some practical diets has improved interior egg quality. Certain crude ingredients contain factors that counteract toxicity of mineral elements. Linseed meal contains an organic factor that counteracts selenium toxicity, and cottonseed meal and alfalfa meal contain a factor(s) that counteracts vanadium toxicity.

Responses to sources of unidentified growth factors have been variable. Some research information has indicated no response. Generally, younger animals show a greater response than older ones. Suggestions have been made that this variation in response may be due to (1) subclinical infections, (2) carry-over effects, (3) interactions with temperature or humidity, or (4) amino acid balance. Most nutritionists still incorporate some of the products containing unidentified factors in diets for young birds and breeders.

ANTIBIOTICS

Some antibiotics (although not nutrients in the sense that they are required by the bird) stimulate growth and improve efficiency of feed conversion under most conditions when added to the diet at low concentrations (usually 1 to 10 mg/kg of diet and sometimes as high as 50 mg for young birds, depending on the antibiotic). They are accordingly classified as additives and as growth promotants. Egg production is also frequently improved by additions of antibiotics. It is not clearly understood why antibiotics stimulate growth and under what conditions they may do so. It is assumed that stimulus to growth of the host results from either suppression of microorganisms with adverse effects or encouragement of others with desirable effects. It is known that the wall of the intestine is thinner when antibiotics are fed to young chicks.

There is some concern that feeding of low concentrations of antibiotics may favor proliferation of antibiotic-resistant microorganisms with serious consequences when antibiotics are required for disease control in either man or domestic animals. However, the extent to which low-level antibiotic feeding constitutes a public health hazard is not well-defined. Constraints on the use of particular antibiotics permitted for use in poultry feeds varies among countries and is subject to change.

Detailed information on specific antimicrobial agents, levels of usage, and legal requirements for use may be found in the *Feed Additive Compendium* published each year by the Miller Publishing Company, 2501 Wayzata Boulevard, Minneapolis, Minnesota 55440, and in the compendium of *Medicating Ingredient Brochures*, Plant Products Division, Canada Department of Agriculture, Ottawa, Canada.

For official information concerning Food and Drug Administration approval of antibiotics and other animal drugs, the *Code of Federal Regulations* (CFR), Title 21, should be consulted. Title 21 is revised at least once each year as of April 1. The CFR is kept up to date by the individual issues of the *Federal Register*. These two publications must be used together to determine the latest version of any given rule. Title 21 is published in six parts: Part 500-599 covers animal drugs, feeds, and related products and is for sale by the Superintendent of Documents, U.S. Government Printing Office, Washington, D.C. 20402, for $4.00 (1977 price). The *Federal Register* is available from the Superintendent of Documents for $50.00/year, which includes monthly issues of the "List of CFR Sections Affected" and "The *Federal Register* Index."

WATER

Water is not included in the requirement tables but it is a necessary nutritional component. Water is required in the largest amount of all nutrients. It is needed as a solvent, a lubricant, and a temperature control device. A general rule is that the chicken drinks approximately twice as much water by weight as the feed it consumes. As temperature is increased, the consumption of water increases. The figures given in Table 9 were determined for temperatures at about 21°C (70°F). With broilers, consumption will increase about 4 percent for each 1°F above 70°F. Laying hens may consume from 40 to 80 gallons per day/1,000 hens with increases in temperature from a low of 1.0°C (34°F) to 32°C (90°F). Survival under extremely hot conditions is influenced by the ability to consume large quantities of water. This capacity varies from strain to strain.

When water is restored following extended periods (36–60 hours) of water deprivation, a "drunken syndrome" has been observed in young turkeys. While some survive this, others die following the resubmission of water.

The salt content and pH of water may influence the possible use of water-soluble vitamins and certain other water-administered drugs. Turkeys are known to detect extremely minor differences and, on occasion, will not consume medicated water. Yet, if the same medicant is put in some other water supply, the poults readily consume it. The moisture content of the droppings of laying hens may be reduced by giving water on an intermittent schedule.

Certain water supplies contain high levels of sulfur or sulfates, nitrates, and various levels of trace minerals. Generally, these are readily assimilated by the intestine and may be either helpful or detrimental to the animal. For instance, sulfates may supply a needed nutrient in some cases and yet be unpalatable in others. This variation in response is related to dosage.

SIGNS OF NUTRITIONAL DEFICIENCIES IN CHICKENS AND TURKEYS

The material in this section describes and illustrates the common signs of various nutritional deficiencies encountered by poultry. An attempt has been made to summarize briefly the abnormalities observed in the embryo and in the growing bird. The signs or symptoms indicated usually develop only with diets severely deficient in one specific nutrient. In most situations when deficiencies are encountered, however, the diet is not severely deficient and often the signs are caused by multiple deficiencies. Identification of the causes of the symptoms is accordingly extremely difficult. A chronic deficiency may be most difficult to identify and may result in more serious financial loss than an acute problem.

EMBRYONIC SIGNS

Deficiencies of some vitamins and minerals in the breeder diet are carried over to the egg and can result in poor hatchability. The age at which mortality occurs varies with the particular nutrient and with the concentration of the nutrient in the egg. Low maternal carry-over of vitamins and minerals may also be reflected in slow early growth of progeny. Embryonic mortality may occur without gross evidence of cause. The abnormalities shown below, however, have been observed in relation to nutrient deficiency. It should be noted that not all of the signs appear consistently.

GROWING BIRD SIGNS

The signs are listed by categories, and the usual vitamin or mineral deficiency is shown in the right-hand column in Table 10. Specific deficiencies are described in more detail below.

VITAMIN A

Vitamin A is one of the more unstable vitamins. For this reason, most nutritionists recommend that it be included in feeds at levels somewhat above the actual requirement. "Stabilized" vitamin A preparations have been developed for incorporation into feeds and vitamin supplements. Over the years the allowances for vitamin A have been reduced in part because of the improvement in the stability of the vitamin A concentrates.

A deficiency of this vitamin results in reduced weight gains and poor feather formation (Figure 2). Because these general signs are not specific for vitamin A deficiency, signs such as urates in the kidney tubules and

Nutrient	Sign
Vitamin A	Early mortality—failure of development of circulatory system
Vitamin D	Stunting, soft bones
Vitamin E	Late mortality—hemorrhages and disturbances in circulatory system
Riboflavin	Dwarfing, edema, clubbed down—mortality peak in the middle of incubation period
Pantothenic acid	Mortality generally late and without characteristic sign—subcutaneous hemorrhage, abnormal feathering
Biotin	Skeletal deformities including shortened, twisted bones of feet and wings (micromelia), skull deformaties, crooked (parrot) beak, webbing between toes (syndactyly)

Nutrient	Sign
Folacin	Mortality generally late and without characteristic signs—bent tibiotarsus, syndactyly, parrot beak
Vitamin B$_{12}$	Edema, shortening of beak, poor muscle development (myotrophy of legs), perosis, hemorrhages
Manganese	Shortened leg bones, perosis, skull deformation, parrot beak
Zinc	Faulty spine and limb development, caudal part of trunk absent, portions of, or entire, limbs missing, small eyes (microphthalmia), abnormalities of beak and other head structures
Iodine	Enlarged thyroid glands, incomplete closure of navel, prolonged incubation time

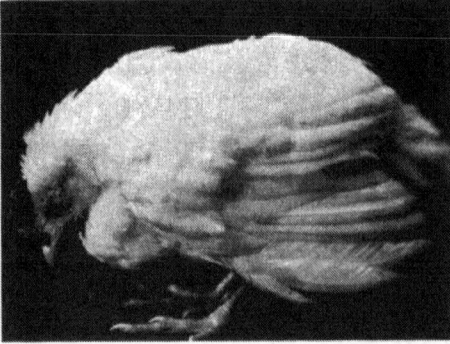

FIGURE 2 An advanced stage of vitamin A deficiency. Note the exudate from the eye and the nostrils and the general ruffled appearance. (Courtesy of Cornell University.)

ureters (Figure 3), keratinization of epithelial tissues (Figure 4), and an ataxia are more reliable as indicators of deficiency. A chronic deficiency in the adult has been referred to as "nutritional roup" because of the discharge from the eyes and nostrils. Lacrimation and, eventually, xerophthalmia develop. In the adult bird, decreased production and even decreased fertility are observed. As is indicated in the text table above, the embryo may also be affected. The involvement of the epithelial tissue also increases susceptibility to infection from parasitic infestations such as coccidiosis and roundworms. It is believed that a deficiency of this vitamin reduces production of antibodies.

Extreme overdosage of vitamin A (retinol) can be toxic in young poults or chicks. With the laying hen, levels over 50,000 IU/kg of diet will decrease the yolk content of

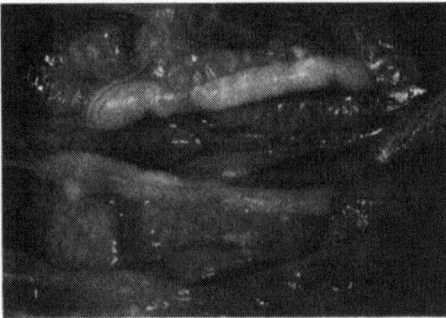

FIGURE 4 An advanced case of vitamin A deficiency showing the pharynx and esophagus studded with pustules. (Courtesy of the University of California.)

xanthophyll-type pigments. Levels two to three times that amount will result in increased blood spots and decreased egg production.

A number of compounds can function as vitamin A. β-Carotene is the most active precursor of vitamin A. Other substances such as cryptoxanthin, α-carotene, and γ-carotene are less potent.

VITAMIN D

Vitamin D is essential for regulation of calcium absorption from the digestive tract and deposition and removal of calcium in the medullary bone. Vitamin D_2 (ergocalciferol) is only about 1/30 to 1/40 as effective for birds as vitamin D_3 (cholecalciferol). Within the last 5 years more active forms of vitamin D have been isolated and synthesized. They are 25-OH vitamin D_3, which is synthesized in the liver, and 1,25-$(OH)_2D_3$, which is produced in the kidney.

A lack of vitamin D in the absence of direct sunlight results in improper bone formation. This condition is commonly called rickets. Chicks deprived of vitamin D

FIGURE 3 Effect of vitamin A deficiency on the kidneys. Note the whitish urate deposits in the kidneys and the enlarged ureters. (Courtesy of the University of Wisconsin.)

stand with "locked hock" joints. These joints become enlarged, and the beak becomes soft and rubbery and can be easily bent (Figure 5). With certain feather color patterns, primarily ermine, an abnormal blackening of the feathers develops. Rib ends may also become beaded, and feathering and growth will be affected adversely.

In laying birds, thin-shelled eggs result, followed by decreased egg production and eventually a high percentage of shell-less eggs. The bones are affected by mineral loss, and birds may lose the use of their legs. Egg size may be affected as well as hatchability. The embryos frequently die at 18 to 19 days, and they may show a short upper mandible or incomplete formation of the base of the beak. Although vitamin D_3 can be toxic at extremely high levels, at least 100 times the requirement level will be tolerated.

VITAMIN E

Chicks deficient in vitamin E may exhibit symptoms of encephalomalacia, exudative diathesis, and muscular dystrophy. The major symptoms of encephalomalacia are sudden prostration, with legs outstretched and toes flexed (Figure 6), and head retraction, frequently with lateral twisting. There is incoordination; the gait is affected before the most severe symptoms are apparent. Upon autopsy, lesions are found in the cerebellum and often in the cerebrum. Necrotic reddish or brownish areas may be detected on the surface of the cerebellum in many chicks. Under some conditions a deficiency of the vitamin results in subcutaneous edema and an edema of the heart and

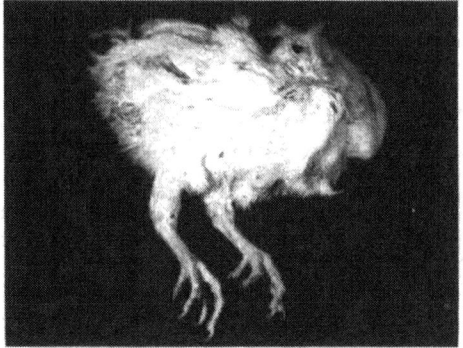

FIGURE 6   α-Tocopherol deficiency in a young chick. Note loss of control of legs and head retraction. (Courtesy of Cornell University.)

pericardium. Exudative diathesis, in chicks, is a severe edema that results from a marked increase in capillary permeability. There is an accumulation of an exudate with a protein pattern similar to blood serum or plasma, primarily in the area of the breast under the skin. A characteristic greenish discoloration results from hemoglobin degeneration. Myopathy (nutritional muscular dystrophy) occurs in chicks when vitamin E deficiency and a sulfur amino acid deficiency occur simultaneously. This condition is characterized by degeneration of the muscle fibers of the breast, but degeneration may also occur in the leg muscles.

Selenium will prevent exudative diathesis and is completely effective in preventing muscular dystrophy when added to the diet in the presence of a low level of vitamin E. Nutritional muscular dystrophy in vitamin E-deficient chicks may be prevented by cystine. The latter illustrates the interrelationship of vitamin E, selenium, and cystine in chick nutrition.

In mature fowl, prolonged vitamin E deficiency brings about permanent sterility in the male and reproductive failure in the female. In females, egg production apparently is not affected by a vitamin E deficiency, but hatchability is markedly reduced. The early classical studies indicated that a deficiency of vitamin E resulted in high mortality from circulatory failure during the first 4 days of incubation. Subsequent studies have shown, however, that high mortality may occur during the last days of incubation and continue after hatching.

Vitamin E deficiency in poults causes nutritional myopathy, characterized by lesions in the muscular wall of the gizzard, appearing as circumscribed gray areas that often are of firmer texture than normal muscle. In some instances, the lesion appears to be like scar tissue.

There is a bulging of the cornea and a protruding eye in vitamin-E-deficient turkey embryos, with a yellowish-

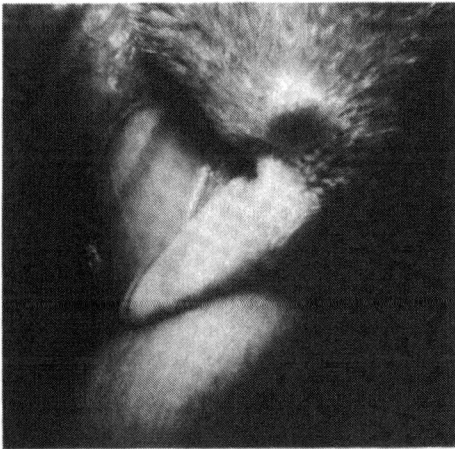

FIGURE 5   Vitamin D deficiency. The beak becomes soft and pliable after 2–3 weeks on a rachitic diet. (Courtesy of the University of Wisconsin.)

white spot between the lens and the cornea at 24–28 days of incubation. Cataracts and hemorrhages occur in the eyes, with a liquefaction of the lens protein.

VITAMIN K

A lack of vitamin K greatly delays the blood-clotting time, and chicks fed a deficient ration may bleed to death from an injury that causes rupture of blood vessels. Hemorrhages may occur subcutaneously, intramuscularly, or intraperitoneally (Figure 7). The hemorrhages vary in extent and appear to be the only symptoms of the deficiency.

Mature birds apparently are not subject to acute vitamin K deficiency, which suggests that microbial synthesis in the intestine provides an adequate source. It has been shown, however, that birds fed a diet low in vitamin K produce eggs that are low in vitamin K. When these eggs are incubated, chicks with very low reserves of vitamin K are hatched. As a consequence, the chicks may bleed to death from an injury as slight as that caused by wing banding.

Antimicrobial agents such as sulfaquinoxaline and other drugs that suppress vitamin K synthesis by bacteria in the intestine may increase the dietary vitamin K requirement up to 10 times that which may be needed in the absence of such drugs.

Excesses of arsanilic acid (0.02 percent) in the hens' diet will also cause bleeding and death when the chicks

are wing banded. Additions of 0.01 percent will increase clotting time in 4-week-old chicks. Both conditions are corrected by vitamin K additions.

THIAMINE

Day-old chicks, mature chickens, and turkeys placed on a thiamine-deficient diet develop polyneuritis within 9–12 days. Early signs are lethargy and head tremors. In the acute stage of polyneuritis, the chicks show a retraction of the head over the back (Figure 8). Other signs are loss of appetite, emaciation, general weakness, and often convulsions.

Grain and grain by-products are good sources of thiamine, and with grain-based poultry diets thiamine deficiency would not be expected to occur. Infection of grain with certain molds may result in destruction of thiamine. Stability can be a problem in purified diets.

RIBOFLAVIN

A lack of riboflavin in the diet of young chicks results in diarrhea, retardation of growth, and leg paralysis of the type described as curled-toe paralysis. The chicks characteristically walk on their hocks with toes curling inward (Figure 9). Chicks fed a diet only slightly deficient in riboflavin often recover spontaneously. In the early stage the condition is curable, but when it becomes acute it is not. In severe cases of deficiency the brachial and sciatic nerves become much enlarged and softened. Some birds may show paralytic symptoms in which they walk on their hocks without the toes being curled. The carriage of the bird in walking and standing may be modified so that instead of being erect the bird carries its head, tail, and wings low.

FIGURE 7 Generalized hemorrhage in a young chick caused by a vitamin K deficiency. (Courtesy of Cornell University.)

FIGURE 8 Head retraction caused by a deficiency of thiamine. (Courtesy of the University of Wisconsin.)

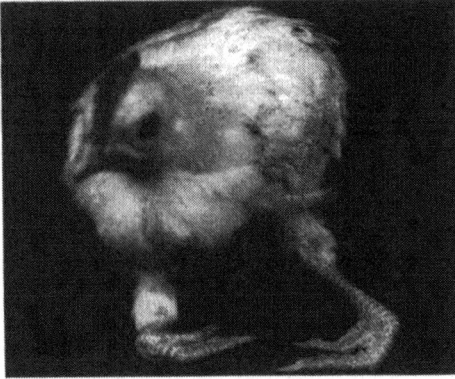

FIGURE 9   Riboflavin deficiency in a young chick. Note the curled toes and tendency to squat on hocks. (Courtesy of Cornell University.)

FIGURE 10   Effect of niacin deficiency on chick growth. (Courtesy of the University of Wisconsin.)

Riboflavin deficiency in breeding hens results in poor hatchability. The requirement for hatchability is considerably higher than that for egg production and maintenance of health.

Embryos that fail to hatch because of riboflavin deficiency are dwarfed and show a high incidence of edema, degeneration of the Wolffian bodies, and a characteristically defective down development termed "clubbed" down. On a ration moderately deficient in riboflavin many chick embryos die during the second week of incubation.

NIACIN

A deficiency of niacin in the diet of chicks results in "black tongue," a condition characterized by inflammation of the tongue and mouth cavity. Beginning at about 2 weeks of age, the entire mouth cavity, as well as the upper part of the esophagus, becomes distinctly inflamed, growth is retarded, and feed consumption is reduced. Poor feather development and occasionally scaly dermatitis of the feet and skin are also observed (Figure 10).

Turkey poults fed a diet deficient in niacin develop a hock disorder similar to perosis. The same condition occurs, but somewhat less frequently, in chicks. Compared to the chick, the turkey poult, duckling, pheasant chick, and gosling have higher requirements for niacin. The higher needs of these species for the vitamin and the all-too-frequent use of a chick starter or growing diet may result in the development of leg weakness.

The niacin in cereal grains and by-products is virtually unavailable and should not be included in the available niacin calculation.

BIOTIN

Biotin deficiency in chicks results in a dermatitis somewhat similar to that observed in pantothenic acid deficiency. Considerable variation in time of appearance of symptoms has been noted. The bottoms of the feet become rough and calloused, and hemorrhagic cracks appear (Figure 11). The toes may become necrotic and slough off, but the tops of the feet and the legs usually show only a dry scaliness. Mandibular lesions first appear in the corners of the mouth and spread to include the area around the beak. Eyelids eventually become swollen and stick together. In contradistinction to these symptoms, the lesions in pantothenic acid deficiency are first evident in the corners of the mouth and eyes, and only in extreme cases do the lesions of the feet become severe.

FIGURE 11   Biotin deficiency. Note the severe lesions on the bottom of the feet. (Courtesy of the University of Wisconsin.)

Biotin has been reported necessary for the prevention of perosis in chicks and turkeys. In poults, the common symptoms are broken flight feathers, bending of the metatarsus, and dermatitis of the footpads and toes, base of beak, eye ring, and vent.

Feeding mature fowl a biotin-deficient ration causes reduced egg hatchability, but egg production is not usually affected. This indicates that the requirement of biotin for producing hatching eggs is higher than that for maintaining good health and egg production. Dermatitis like that observed in chicks fed biotin-deficient diets has not been reported in hens. Evidence of biotin deficiency in embryos includes parrot beak, chondrodystrophy, micromelia, and syndactyly.

Responses to biotin have been much easier to demonstrate with diets high in wheat and barley than with diets high in corn. This is because the biotin in wheat and barley is relatively unavailable. In certain instances it has been stated that supplementary biotin is of benefit to young turkeys fed a corn-based diet. The reason for this may relate to the formation of a biotin antimetabolite by molds. Avidin, a protein in uncooked egg white, has the capacity to bind biotin and render it unavailable nutritionally, and therefore other instances in nature of the production of biotin antimetabolites would not seem unlikely. Biotin deficiency has also been induced by oxidation accompanying development of rancidity in fat.

PANTOTHENIC ACID

Pantothenic acid deficiency in young chicks results in retarded growth and extremely ragged feather development. Within 12 to 14 days a viscous exudate causes the eyelids to become granular and stick together. Crusty scabs appear at the corners of the mouth (Figure 12) and

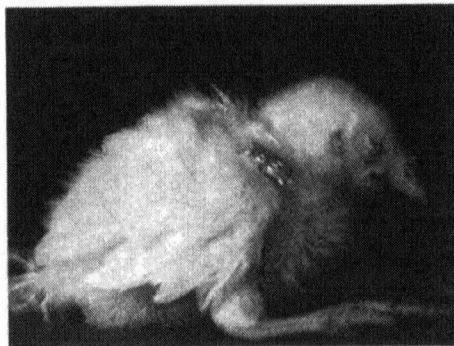

FIGURE 12 An advanced stage of pantothenic acid deficiency. Note the lesions at the corners of the mouth and on the eyelids and feet. (Courtesy of Cornell University.)

around the vent. Dermatitis of the feet has been observed, but the lesions are seldom as severe as those brought about by biotin deficiency. Liver damage and changes in the spinal cord are sometimes found postmortem. Such lesions have not been observed in adult fowl, but pantothenic acid deficiency does result in lowered egg hatchability.

When a diet somewhat low in pantothenic acid is fed to breeder hens, egg production may continue normally. However, the resulting newly hatched chick is too weak to eat and dies. Ultimately, hatchability declines and the chick fails to emerge from the egg. The mortality peak occurs during the last few days of the hatching period.

An interesting set of circumstances led to this syndrome in Pennsylvania in 1954 and in New Jersey 2 years later. When newly hatched chicks were placed under brooders, most of them promptly died. It was possible to completely remedy the difficulty by administering a vitamin mixture subcutaneously. Eventually it was found that pantothenic acid alone would alleviate the condition. The interpretation as to why the breeder diet suddenly became marginal in pantothenic acid involved the use of artificially dried corn (heating destroys pantothenic acid) and the omission of milk by-products from the diet. The breeder diet was not supplemented with pantothenic acid.

CHOLINE

Growth retardation and perosis are induced by choline deficiency in chicks, poults, and ducklings. Most recent evidence indicates that choline is synthesized by mature chickens in quantities adequate for egg production.

The choline requirement of the laying hen may be influenced by the amount of choline fed during the growing period. Laying hens appear capable of synthesizing considerable amounts of choline. There is little evidence that practical pullet growing rations or laying rations require supplementation with choline. Additions of choline may, however, be a factor in egg size for quail, and the dietary requirement of growing quail appears to be higher than that for chicks or poults.

VITAMIN B₆

Chicks fed a diet deficient in vitamin B_6 show a lack of appetite and a slow rate of growth. Nervous symptoms develop, which include abnormal excitement, uncontrollable forced running movements accompanied by constant cheeping, and convulsions during which the chick may rest on its breast, raise its feet off the floor and flap its wings or fall on its side, or roll over on its back and rapidly paddle its feet. The head often retracts and sometimes moves convulsively in an up-and-down movement with the neck extended or twisted. Violent convulsions cause complete exhaustion and may terminate in death. A sign of borderline deficiency is severe perosis.

Vitamin B_6 deficiency in mature birds is characterized

by loss of appetite and a consequent rapid decline in weight. Egg production and hatchability are reduced, and death ultimately occurs.

FOLACIN

Folacin deficiency in young chicks results in retarded growth, poor feathering, and loss of feather pigmentation. These symptoms are accompanied by an anemia characterized by a reduction in the number of red blood cells and in the level of hemoglobin. The red cells are larger than normal, and the hemoglobin content of the cells is increased. The red blood cells are malformed.

In breeding chickens, folacin deficiency reduces egg production and hatchability. Deficient embryos show bending of the tibiotarsus, mandible defects, syndactyly, and hemorrhages.

Turkey poults deficient in folic acid are quite nervous and exhibit droopy wings, and some have a stiff and extended neck condition called cervical paralysis. Poults showing the latter symptoms usually die within 2 days after visible symptoms appear.

Turkey breeder hens with folacin deficiency show normal egg production with reduced hatchability. Increased embryo mortality occurs at 26-28 days, just prior to the normal hatching time. There are abnormalities including micromelia, twisted hocks, mandibular defects, enlarged fluid-filled gizzards, hemorrhages, and edema.

Research has shown that in certain instances folic acid added to natural diets improves growth and prevents cervical paralysis in young turkeys. Folacin is now commonly added to turkey breeder and prestarter diets. It is also often added to chicken starting and breeding diets, especially when broiler chicks are involved.

VITAMIN B_{12}

Vitamin B_{12} is essential for hatchability, chick growth, and prevention of gizzard erosion. There is carry-over of the vitamin from the dam to the chick, and mortality may be high among chicks deficient in the vitamin at hatching time. Deficient embryos show hemorrhages and edema. Fatty heart, liver, and kidneys may occur, and perosis may also be involved in the deficiency syndrome. Marginal levels of the vitamin will produce poorly feathered chicks.

CALCIUM AND PHOSPHORUS

Bone formation is highly dependent on adequate supplies of calcium, phosphorus, and vitamin D. A deficiency of any one of these results in rickets, but effects on blood may vary, depending on the factor that is lacking. Retarded growth is also a symptom of calcium and phosphorus deficiency, which, when it becomes acute,

leads to death. Rib deformation is caused by the occurrence of small fractures.

Cage-layer fatigue has been reported as a symptom of phosphorus deficiency. However, there is evidence that the condition is not due to this factor alone.

Hens that succumb to cage-layer fatigue (Figure 13) are usually in full production. Affected birds are paralyzed and cannot rise from a recumbent position. If they are left in the cages, they die of starvation. When removed from the cages and placed on the floor, severely affected birds lie with their legs extended laterally or anteriorly, while less severely affected birds rest on their hocks. Frequently they will recover when placed on the floor.

The sternum and rib bones of affected birds are frequently deformed, and all bones are easily broken. Most evident are fractures of the fourth and fifth thoracic vertebrae and an associated compression and degeneration of the spinal cord, which is believed to be the cause of the paralysis noted in this condition.

MAGNESIUM

When fed a diet totally deficient in magnesium, chicks grow slowly for about 1 week and then stop growing and become lethargic. Chicks fed diets marginal in magnesium may grow quite well but will exhibit depressed plasma magnesium levels and symptoms of neuromuscular hyperirritability when disturbed. Chicks show a brief convulsion and then go into a comatose state from which they usually recover, but sometimes death results. A magnesium deficiency in laying hens results in a rapid decline in egg production, reduced magnesium level in the blood, and a marked withdrawal of magnesium from

FIGURE 13 Cage fatigue paralysis. When condition progresses, bird will lie on its side. (Courtesy of the University of Wisconsin.)

bones. Raising either the calcium or phosphorus content of the diet accentuates a magnesium deficiency in chicks fed a diet marginal in the element.

MANGANESE

Manganese deficiency in the diet of growing chicks and poults results in perosis or slipped tendon (Figure 14). As has been mentioned, perosis may also be caused by a deficiency of choline or biotin.

Perosis is a malformation of the bones. The symptoms usually observed are swelling and flattening of the hock joint, with subsequent slipping of the Achilles tendon from its condyles. The tibia and the tarsometatarsus may exhibit bending near the hock joint and lateral rotation. One or both legs may be affected. A shortening and thickening of the long bones of the wings and legs are also observed. The disorder, insofar as manganese is concerned, is aggravated by excessive quantities of calcium and phosphorus in the ration.

In laying and breeding birds, manganese deficiency results in lowered egg production and hatchability and reduced eggshell strength. In many cases, embryos that die as a result of manganese deficiency exhibit chondrodystrophy, a condition characterized by a parrot-like beak, wiry down, and shortening of the long bones. This condition is not, however, specific for manganese deficiency.

CHLORIDE

The chloride deficiency symptoms in chicks include extremely poor growth, high mortality, hemoconcentration, nervous symptoms, and a reduced blood chloride level. Chloride-deficient chicks show a typical nervous

FIGURE 14 Perosis or slipped tendon resulting from a deficiency of manganese. A deficiency of either choline or biotin may also result in perosis. (Courtesy of Cornell University.)

condition resembling tetany and fall forward with legs extended to the rear when stimulated by a sharp noise.

COPPER

Copper deficiency in poultry causes a microcytic, hypochromic anemia. Various bone deformities and depigmentation in New Hampshire chicks are also observed. Dissecting aneurysm of the aorta occurs in deficient chicks because copper is necessary for amino oxidase, an enzyme needed for the cross-linking of lysine in the elastins of the aorta. Copper deficiency in turkey poults results in a marked cardiac hypertrophy.

IODINE

Iodine deficiency results in goiter, an enlargement of the thyroid gland. The gland increases to many times its normal size, and histological examination shows hyperplasia and an absence of colloid. Iodine deficiency in the breeding hen results in reduced iodine content of the egg and, consequently, decreased hatchability. Embryos exhibit a thyroidal enlargement.

IRON

Iron deficiency in chicks and turkey poults results in a microcytic, hypochromic anemia. In red-feathered chickens complete depigmentation of the feathers occurs in iron deficiency.

POTASSIUM

There is high mortality and retarded growth in chicks fed a diet deficient in potassium. It is not necessary to add potassium to practical feed formulations since such formulas generally contain about 1 percent potassium.

SODIUM

A deficiency of sodium in chicken diets results in decreased egg production, poor growth, and cannibalism. Frequently the sodium level is reduced to minimal levels to control the moisture level in the feces.

SELENIUM

Selenium is closely associated with vitamin E and other antioxidants in practical feeding of poultry. The main deficiency symptom displayed by selenium-deficient chicks is exudative diathesis (Figure 15). With a severe deficiency of selenium as might be obtained with a purified diet, or with grains produced on low-selenium

ment of some of the barbules and barbicels (see Figures 16 and 17).

The hock joint may become enlarged. The long bones of the legs and wings also become shortened and thickened with a deficiency. A zinc deficiency in the

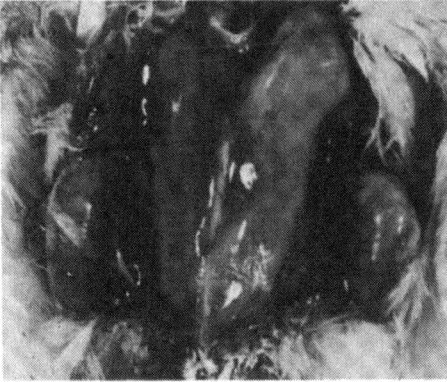

FIGURE 15 Exudative diathesis produced by a deficiency of selenium and vitamin E. (Courtesy of Cornell University.)

soils, the growth rate will also be reduced and the mortality increased even in the presence of adequate vitamin E. Selenium is also required to prevent myopathies of the gizzard and heart in turkeys. Pancreatic fibrosis and a reduction in lipase, trypsinogen, and chymotrypsinogen have also been associated with the deficiency. Selenium is also a structural component of glutathione peroxidase. The amount of selenium in a feedstuff is greatly altered by the amount and availability of the selenium in the soil. For instance, grains or milling by-products from sections of North and South Dakota contain several times more selenium than grains from Ohio or New York.

It is possible, on the other hand, to have grains from isolated areas of South Dakota that are high enough in selenium to produce toxic effects in chicks. Excess selenium will reduce hatchability and will cause a number of embryonic abnormalities if fed at levels greater than 5 ppm. Other symptoms resulting from the feeding of high levels of seleniferous grains are impaired growth, ruffled feathers, nervousness, and delayed sexual maturity.

ZINC

Zinc is involved in a long list of physiological functions. Because of this, many studies have been made to determine the primary defects responsible for the deficiency symptoms shown by poultry. As with many deficiencies, growth is retarded and feather development abnormal. Feather fraying occurs near the ends of the feathers. The severity of the fraying varies from almost no feathers on the wings and tail to only slight defects in the develop-

FIGURE 16 Severe zinc deficiency produced with a casein diet at age 5 weeks. (Courtesy of the University of Wisconsin.)

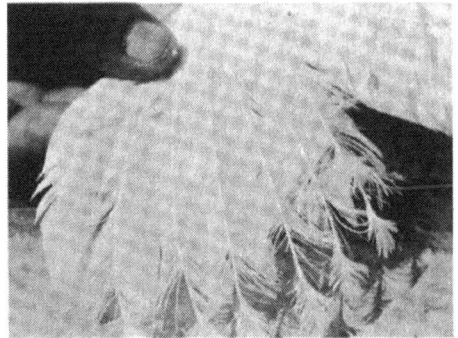

FIGURE 17 Moderate zinc deficiency produces frayed feathers in egg strain pullets at 3 weeks of age. Incidence is 5–10 percent with 35–40 ppm zinc in diet. (Courtesy of the University of Wisconsin.)

breeder diet will reduce egg production and hatchability. The embryos produced in deficient eggs show a wide variety of skeletal abnormalities involving the head, limbs, and vertebrae.

Injections of rather minute amounts (2 mg of zinc) will kill day-old chicks or embryos within hours. This will occur when the injection is by the subcutaneous or intraperitoneal routes, as well as intrayolk. However, much higher levels can be fed in a water solution over a 24-hour period without harmful effects. Supplying zinc in the water for only 3 days will prevent feather fraying in chicks fed practical diets containing 35 ppm zinc.

TOXIC LEVELS OF
INORGANIC ELEMENTS

Table 11 summarizes current information on toxic levels of inorganic elements for poultry. Toxicity as defined here is any adverse effect on the performance of the bird. Reduced growth rate is the most common physiological effect used to indicate at what level a particular mineral is toxic. Although most of the information represents experiments in which the element was added in the form of inorganic compounds, organic compounds served as the source of the element in some of the reports. For instance, information on toxicity of arsenic came from studies in which arsenicals were fed. Toxicity is influenced by the form of the element. For example, methyl mercury is considerably more toxic than inorganic mercury. Toxicity is also markedly influenced by composition of the diet, particularly with respect to the content of other mineral elements. Selenium included in the diet at a level of 10 ppm reduces growth rate, but, when fed in combination with 1,000 ppm silver, a level as high as 40 ppm did not reduce growth rate. Copper included at a level of 800 ppm in a practical turkey diet was not toxic, but 50 ppm of copper included in a purified diet reduced growth rate. In many cases a high dietary level of one element will antagonize another element, resulting in a physiological deficiency of elements essential for the animal. Copper added as an antifungal agent in feeds could precipitate a molybdenum deficiency if the diet is marginal in the latter element. Reports of field cases in Australia have indicated such a deficiency in breeder hens fed natural feeds. Because of these factors affecting the quantity of an element needed to produce a toxicity, different observers will reach different conclusions about what constitutes a toxic effect of a specific element. For these reasons, original reports are cited for the individual figures in the table for the convenience of the reader wishing to consult them. Birds can tolerate levels up to those shown in the table without harmful effects.

DAILY NUTRIENT REQUIREMENTS FOR EGG-TYPE AND BROILER-TYPE CHICKENS

The daily nutrient requirements for light and heavy breeds of chickens presented in Tables 12 and 13 were computed from values given in Tables 1, 2, 3, 14, and 15. It is hoped that these values will be of use in studies on comparative nutrition as well as for developing feeding programs using daily intake as an important consideration. Expressing the nutrient requirements on a daily-intake basis will assist in interpretation of basic relationships between nutritional requirements for the various species and types of farm animals.

FEED REQUIREMENTS FOR POULTRY OF VARIOUS AGES AND SPECIES

The information in Table 14 reflects feed requirements for laying hens of various weights and percent productions. These are calculated values, but they have been confirmed many times under average temperature conditions. Again, consumption is affected by the factors indicated above.

Data showing the quantity of feed needed for broiler-type and Leghorn-type chickens to attain certain weights are given in Table 15. Typical weights at various ages are also indicated. Considerable variation from the figures given may result because of strain variation, feed restriction procedures, feed wastage, or variation in the quality of feed or energy content of the diet. Ambient temperature will also influence the results. The same information has been developed for turkeys and ducks and is presented in Tables 16 and 17.

22

FEEDING SYSTEMS AND FEED RESTRICTION

Under most conditions poultry are provided with feed and water on an *ad libitum* or free-choice basis. However, restriction of feed intake or limitations on energy, protein, or amino acid intake by variations in feed formulation can be used to retard growth and development of pullets and to prevent overconsumption that results in obesity in laying and breeding hens.

It has become common practice to restrict meat-type chicks to approximately 70 percent of full feed during the period from 4 to 24 weeks of age. Such a restriction is commonly accomplished by careful distribution of a known amount of feed to the growing flock every other day. Meat-type breeder hens are continued on a program of feed restriction after 24 weeks of age with the objective of limiting the hens to about 85 percent of full feed. This objective is usually achieved by careful distribution of a known amount of feed each day. Feeding schedules that permit this degree of restriction are available through the primary broiler breeder organizations.

The use of low-protein and/or amino-acid-imbalanced diets fed on an *ad libitum* basis has also been shown to retard pullet development. Likewise, low-energy diets formulated with large amounts of low-energy ingredients have been used to restrict pullet growth and sexual maturity. These programs are in very limited use because of problems associated with formulation and feed costs.

Currently, little interest exists in restricted feeding of egg-production-type pullets during the growing period because problems with early sexual maturity and feed consumption are usually solved by lighting restriction during growth from 6 to 20 weeks of age. More interest has been shown recently in the modification of feeding programs for egg-type pullets and hens after the time when maximum egg production is reached. There is little doubt that some laying flocks will consume excess feed during egg production with resultant obesity, which may contribute to induction of the fatty liver syndrome. Feed efficiency is also reduced under these circumstances. Limiting feed intake to about 90 percent of full feed

seems to be desirable when overconsumption is a problem. Data on feed consumption in individual flocks along with information on body weight of the hens, temperature, and rate of egg production may be used to decide what degree of feed restriction may be desirable. Some commercial interest also exists in modifying the ratio of energy to other nutrients in laying diets to compensate for changes in temperature that alter feed intake and to compensate for changes in egg production with age. Such feeding programs have been referred to as "phase feeding" or "tailored feeding."

After a period of 8 to 12 months of egg production, some poultrymen induce forced molting in their flocks as a means for recycling their hens for another period of egg production and improving egg quality. Forced molting requires abrupt changes in the feeding program. All sources of drinking water are removed for 2 or 3 days and all feed is withheld for 3 to 5 days to induce molting. Drinking water is returned after the above indicated period, but feed is limited to 3 or 4 kg per 100 birds per day for the next 6 to 8 days. Usually the restriction of feed and water is coupled with an abrupt reduction in lighting of the flock from about 14 to 6 hours per day for 5 to 6 weeks. The combination of feed and water restriction and reduction in time of lighting (hours of light per day) usually results in a heavy molt in most of the hens, with a return to egg production when the period of lighting is increased. Many egg producers find that the recycled flock produces, for a period of time, large eggs of better interior and exterior quality.

Growth restriction of potential turkey breeders usually does not improve reproductive performance, and under some conditions it may prove to be detrimental. However, the use of "holding feeds" for potential turkey breeders is commonly practiced. These feeds are usually designed at medium energy levels to stabilize development and weight gains after market age. Care should be taken to see that vitamin and mineral fortification of holding rations is adequate for breeder performance.

STANDARD REFERENCE DIETS FOR CHICKS

Many laboratories using the chick as an experimental animal for a variety of purposes require a nutritionally complete standard reference diet. Such a diet ensures that adequate nutrition is available to chicks being used for studies in microbiology, physiology, pathology, behavior, biochemistry, and other sciences. The diets shown in the table below meet the nutrient requirements of meat- or broiler-type chicks for rapid growth and develoment. Vitamin and trace mineral levels have been increased above requirement levels to compensate for some instability due to storage and variability in composition of natural ingredients.

Ingredient	Practical Diet[a] (g/kg)	Purified Diet (g/kg)
Ground yellow corn (8.8% protein) (g)	580	—
Soybean meal (48.5% protein) (g)	350	—
Corn oil (g)	30	30
Calcium carbonate (g)	10	
Dicalcium phosphate (g)	20	—
Iodized salt (g)	5	5
DL-Methionine (g)	2.5	3
Choline chloride (50%) (g)	1.5	1.5
Isolated soy protein (g)		300
Glucose or dextrinized starch (g)		561
Mineral mixture[b] (g)		50
Cellulose (g)		50
1,2-Dihydro-6-ethoxy-2,2,4-trimethyl-quinoline (ethoxyquin) (mg)	125.0	125.0
Manganese sulfate·[ca.]5H$_2$O (mg)	170.0	400.0
Zinc sulfate· H$_2$O (mg)	110.0	200.0
Ferric citrate· [ca.]5H$_2$O (mg)	500.0	500.0
Copper sulfate· 5H$_2$O (mg)	16.0	16.0
Sodium selenite (mg)	0.2	0.2
Thiamine-HCl (mg)	1.8	1.8
Riboflavin (mg)	3.6	3.6
Calcium pantothenate (mg)	10.0	10.0
Niacin (mg)	25.0	25.0
Pyridoxine-HCl (mg)	3.0	3.0
Folacin (mg)	0.55	0.55
Biotin (mg)	0.15	0.15
Vitamin B$_{12}$(mg)	0.01	0.01
Vitamin K-1 (mg)	0.55	0.55
Vitamin A (units)	1,500	5,000
Vitamin D$_3$ (units)	400	400
Vitamin E (units)	10	10

[a] Animal Nutrition Research Council Reference Chick Diet.
[b] Mineral mixture to provide 15 g CaCO$_3$, 14 g Ca$_3$(PO$_4$)$_2$, 9 g K$_2$HPO$_4$, 7.2 g Na$_2$HPO$_4$, 5 g M$_g$SO$_4$·7H$_2$O, 0.05 g KI, 0.02 g NaBr, and 0.01 g Na$_2$MO$_4$.

AVERAGE COMPOSITION OF FEEDSTUFFS USED IN POULTRY DIETS

The requirement figures for any species of livestock must be correlated with the amount of the nutrient thought to be found in the ingredients fed. If the values found in the composition tables are 10 percent too high, then a deficiency could theoretically be noted even though, by calculation, the level in the diet should meet the established requirement.

Therefore, actual determined amounts of the nutrients in each ingredient used in a poultry formula or absolutely accurate table figures would be desired. However, in practice, because of varied composition, tables must be averages, and actual analysis can only rarely be done before the diet is consumed. Composition tables then need to be as accurate as possible.

The values found in Tables 18, 19, 20, and 21 have been obtained from many sources. Major sources of information have been: (1) the *United States-Canadian Tables of Feed Composition*,* (2) the *Atlas of Nutritional Data on United States and Canadian Feeds*,† (3) the data bank on composition of feedstuffs maintained at Utah State University, Logan, Utah, under the direction of L. E. Harris, International Feedstuffs Institute, (4) the trade associations for the various special products, (5) commercial feed companies, and (6) values obtained from individual scientists at the agricultural experiment stations.

The various laboratories do not agree on certain values. An attempt has been made in this publication to use values near the midrange. For instance, even a major ingredient in the diet such as corn will vary from 8 to 11 percent protein on an "as-fed" or "as-is" basis. This will be true even with a standardized moisture content. Fortunately, differences in values for more exotic ingredients do not greatly affect the overall content of a feed, because only 1 to 3 percent of these materials are gen-

erally used. When large amounts of one of the unusual ingredients are used in a feed, more accurate analysis is recommended.

Ingredients vary in composition because of variety, soil type, fertilization rate, climatic conditions, and length of storage. Variations in analytical procedures also affect results.

There are a number of blanks in the tables. While, in a few instances, values from only one or two analyses have been reported, generally the subcommittee feels that this should not be done. At the same time, they recognize that individual feed formulators must either place a value in their computer data bank or record the amount as a zero. As with the "estimated" requirement values, the subcommittee thinks that the combined judgment of the subcommittee members may be better in most instances than the judgment of individuals pressed to insert a number in their program for the computer.

The nutrient contents are all expressed on an "as-fed" or "as-is" basis. The percent dry matter, however, is shown in the tables. In addition, the International Feed Number from the *Atlas* or from the data bank maintained by L. E. Harris is given. The number selected was usually the most general term available and would be applicable in most situations. For instance, "oats grain. 4-03-309," was used rather than either "oats grain, gr 2 U.S. Mn wt. 32 lbs. per bushel, 4-03-316," or "oats grain, mn 80% oats, mx 15% fiber, 10% wild oats, 4-03-328," because more analyses were carried in the data bank. The identification number given here is the Association of American Feed Control Officials (AAFCO) number for oats.

The AAFCO terms for ingredients are used except for some that have not as yet been named by this organization. An attempt has also been made to include in the list some other ingredients used rather frequently by research laboratories.

In Table 18 the energy level, protein, calcium, and phosphorus are shown toward the left-hand side to make it less difficult to stay with one horizontal line. The trace minerals are listed next, and the vitamins last. The term

*Publication 1684, National Academy of Sciences, Washington, D.C.
†Publication 1919, National Academy of Sciences, Washington, D.C.

pyridoxine, perhaps, should be listed as "Vitamin B_6 activity," but the terminology becomes somewhat irrelevant since laboratories use pyridoxine as a standard.

The amino acids in Table 19 are in alphabetical order except for glycine and serine, methionine and cystine, and phenylalanine and tyrosine. These are placed in pairs to make it easier for those using the table to make the appropriate calculations.

The values in the fat and fatty acid table (Table 20) were obtained from the literature and from the laboratories of individuals on this subcommittee.

The values shown in the mineral table (Table 21) were obtained from the various manufacturers of these products and from the NRC publication *Feed Phosphorus Shortage: Levels and Sources of Phosphorus Recommended for Livestock and Poultry.*

MAJOR
TABLES

TABLE 1 Protein and Amino Acid Requirements of Broilers

Nutrient	Broilers					
	0-3 Weeks		3-6 Weeks		6-9 Weeks	
	%[a]	g/Mcal	%[a]	g/Mcal	%[a]	g/Mcal
Protein	23.0	—	20.0	—	18	—
Arginine	1.44	4.50	1.20	3.75	1.00	3.13
Glycine + serine	1.50	4.69	1.00	3.13	0.70	2.19
Histidine	0.35	1.09	0.30	0.94	0.26	0.81
Isoleucine	0.80	2.50	0.70	2.19	0.60	1.88
Leucine	1.35	4.22	1.18	3.69	1.00	3.13
Lysine	1.20	3.75	1.00	3.13	0.85	2.66
Methionine + cystine	0.93	2.90	0.72	2.25	0.60	1.88
Methionine	0.50	1.56	0.38	1.19	0.32	1.00
Phenylalanine + tyrosine	1.34	4.19	1.17	3.66	1.00	3.13
Phenylalanine	0.72	2.25	0.63	1.97	0.54	1.69
Threonine	0.75	2.34	0.65	2.03	0.56	1.75
Tryptophan	0.23	0.72	0.20	0.63	0.17	0.53
Valine	0.82	2.56	0.72	2.25	0.62	1.94

[a]Requirement for diets containing 3,200 kcal metabolizable energy per kg.

TABLE 2 Protein and Amino Acid Requirements of Egg-Type and Meat-Type Chickens

Nutrient	Replacement Pullets[a] (Egg- or Meat-Type)						Laying and Breeding Hens[b] (Egg- or Meat-Type)	
	0-6 Weeks		6-14 Weeks		14-20 Weeks		% of Diet[c]	Daily Intake per Hen[d] (mg)
	%	g/Mcal	%	g/Mcal	%	g/Mcal		
Protein	18	—	15	—	12	—	15	16,500
Arginine	1.00	3.45	0.83	2.86	0.67	2.31	0.8	880
Glycine + serine	0.70	2.42	0.58	2.00	0.47	1.62	0.5	550
Histidine	0.26	0.90	0.22	0.76	0.17	0.59	0.22	240
Isoleucine	0.60	2.07	0.50	1.73	0.40	1.38	0.5	550
Leucine	1.00	3.45	0.83	2.86	0.67	2.31	1.2	1,320
Lysine	0.85	2.93	0.60	2.07	0.45	1.55	0.60[e]	660[e]
Methionine + cystine	0.60	2.07	0.50	1.73	0.40	1.38	0.50	550
Methionine	0.32	1.10	0.27	0.93	0.21	0.72	0.27	300
Phenylalanine + tyrosine	1.00	3.45	0.83	2.86	0.67	2.31	0.8	880
Phenylalanine	0.54	1.86	0.45	1.55	0.36	1.24	0.4	440
Threonine	0.56	1.93	0.47	1.62	0.37	1.28	0.4	440
Tryptophan	0.17	0.59	0.14	0.48	0.11	0.38	0.11	120
Valine	0.62	2.14	0.52	1.79	0.41	1.41	0.5	550

[a]The requirements shown are for reasonable growth and development at 20 weeks of age when rations are fed on an ad libitum basis. Most of the values are not determined but are based on values for young birds and extrapolated for the older birds. Values under percent are based on 2,900 kcal of metabolizable energy/kg.
[b]The values in lightface type are estimates. See page 1.
[c]Based on 2,850 kcal of metabolizable energy/kg diet.
[d]Based on a feed consumption of 110 g per day.
[e]Determined with corn-soybean meal diets. The requirement may be higher on wheat-based diets.

TABLE 3   Vitamin, Linoleic Acid, and Mineral Requirements of Chickens[a]
(in Percentage or Amount per Kilogram of Feed)

Nutrient	Starting Chickens (0–8 Weeks)	Growing Chickens (8-18 Weeks)	Laying Hens	Breeding Hens
Vitamin A activity (IU)	1,500	1,500	4,000	4,000
Vitamin D (ICU)[b]	200	200	500	500
Vitamin E (IU)	10	5	5	10
Vitamin K$_1$ or equivalent activity (mg)	0.5	0.5	0.5	0.5
Thiamine (mg)	1.8	1.3	0.8	0.8
Riboflavin (mg)	3.6	1.8	2.2	3.8
Pantothenic acid (mg)	10	10	2.2	10
Niacin (mg)	27	11	10	10
Pyridoxine (mg)	3	3	3	4.5
Biotin (mg)	0.15	0.10	0.10	0.15
Choline (mg)[c]	1,300	500	500	500
Folacin (mg)[d]	0.55	0.25	0.25	0.35
Vitamin B$_{12}$ (mg)	0.009	0.003	0.003	0.003
Linoleic acid (%)	1.0	0.8	1.0	1.0
Calcium (%)	0.9	0.6	3.25	2.75
Phosphorus (%)[e]	0.7	0.4	0.5	0.5
Potassium (%)	0.2	0.16	0.1	0.1
Sodium (%)	0.15	0.15	0.15	0.15
Chlorine (mg)	800	800	800	800
Copper (mg)	4	3	3	4
Iodine (mg)	0.35	0.35	0.3	0.3
Iron (mg)	80	40	50	80
Magnesium (mg)	600	400	500	500
Manganese (mg)	55	25	25	33
Selenium (mg)	0.1	0.1	0.1	0.1
Zinc (mg)	40	35	50	65

[a]The values in lightface type are estimates.
[b]See text, page 17. These levels of vitamin D are satisfactory when levels of calcium and readily available phosphorus conform to this table.
[c]See text, page 16.
[d]With sucrose, diet requirement is 1.2 mg/kg.
[e]See text, page 7.

TABLE 4   Protein and Amino Acid Requirements of Turkeys[a]

Nutrient	♂ 0-4 ♀ 0-4	4-8 4-8	8-12 8-11	12-16 11-14	16-20 14-17	20-24 17-20	Holding	Breeding Hens
Metabolizable energy[b] (kcal/kg)	2,800	2,900	3,000	3,100	3,200	3,300	2,900	2,900
Protein (%)	28	26	22	19	16.5	14	12	14
Arginine (%)	1.6	1.5	1.25	1.1	0.95	0.8	0.6	0.6
Glycine + serine (%)	1.0	0.9	0.8	0.7	0.6	0.5	0.4	0.5
Histidine (%)	0.58	0.54	0.46	0.39	0.35	0.29	0.25	0.3
Isoleucine (%)	1.1	1.0	0.85	0.75	0.65	0.55	0.45	0.5
Leucine (%)	1.9	1.75	1.5	1.3	1.1	0.95	0.5	0.5
Lysine (%)	1.7	1.6	1.35	1.0	0.80	0.65	0.5	0.6
Methionine + cystine (%)	1.05	0.90	0.75	0.65	0.55	0.45	0.4	0.4
Methionine (%)	0.53	0.45	0.38	0.33	0.28	0.23	0.2	0.2
Phenylalanine + tyrosine (%)	1.8	1.65	1.4	1.2	1.05	0.9	0.8	1.0
Phenylalanine (%)	1.0	0.9	0.8	0.7	0.6	0.5	0.4	0.55
Threonine (%)	1.0	0.93	0.79	0.68	0.59	0.5	0.4	0.45
Tryptophan (%)	0.26	0.24	0.20	0.18	0.15	0.13	0.10	0.13
Valine (%)	1.2	1.1	0.94	0.8	0.7	0.6	0.5	0.58

[a]Values in lightface type are estimates.   [b]Requirement for diets containing the stated levels of metabolizable energy.

TABLE 5 Vitamin, Linoleic Acid, and Mineral
Requirements of Turkeys[a]

Nutrient	% or Amount per kg of Feed		
	0-8 Weeks	8 Weeks[b]	Breeding
Vitamin A (IU)	4,000	4,000	4,000
Vitamin D (ICU)[c]	900	900	900
Vitamin E (IU)	12	10	25
Vitamin K_1 or equivalent activity (mg)	1	0.8	1
Thiamin (mg)	2	2	2
Riboflavin (mg)	3.6	3.0	4
Pantothenic acid (mg)	11	9	16
Niacin (mg)	70	50	30
Vitamin B_6 (mg)	4.5	3.5	4
Biotin (mg)[d]	0.2	0.1	0.15
Choline (mg)	1,900	1,100	1,000
Folacin (mg)	1.0	0.8	1.0
Vitamin B_{12} (mg)	0.003	0.003	0.003
Linoleic acid (%)	1.0	0.8	1.0
Calcium (%)	1.2	0.8	2.25
Phosphorus (%)[e]	0.8	0.7	0.7
Potassium (%)	0.4	0.4	0.4
Sodium (%)	0.15	0.15	0.15
Chlorine (mg)	800	800	800
Copper (mg)	6	4	6
Iodine (mg)	0.4	0.4	0.4
Iron (mg)	60	40	60
Magnesium (mg)	500	500	500
Manganese (mg)	55	25	35
Selenium (mg)	0.2	0.2	0.2
Zinc (mg)	75	40	65

[a]The values in lightface type are estimates.
[b]From 8 weeks to market or prebreeding.
[c]See footnote b, Table 3.
[d]Requirement may be 50 percent greater for wheat- or barley-based diets.
[e]See text, page 7.

TABLE 6   Nutrient Requirements of Pheasants and Quail[a] (in Percentage or Amount per Kilogram of Feed)

Nutrient	Pheasant		Bobwhite Quail		Japanese Quail	
	Starting	Growing (6-20 Weeks)	Starting and Growing	Breeding	Starting and Growing	Breeding
Metabolizable energy (kcal/kg)	2,800	2,700	2,800	2,800	3,000[c]	2,800
Protein (%)	30	16	28[b]	24	24[c]	24
Lysine (%)	1.5	0.8	1.4	0.7	1.4	1.1
Methionine + cystine (%)	1.0	0.6	0.9	0.6	0.75	0.8
Glycine + serine (%)	1.8	1.0	1.6	0.9	1.7	0.9
Vitamin A (IU)	3,000	3,000	3,000	3,000	5,000	5,000
Vitamin D (ICU)	1,200	900	900	900	480	1,200
Riboflavin (mg)	3.5	2.6	3.8	4.0	4.0	4.0
Pantothenic acid (mg)	10	10	12.6	15	10	15
Niacin (mg)	60	40	31	20	40	20
Choline (mg)	1,500	1,000	1,500	1,000	2,000	1,500
Linoleic acid (%)	1.0	1.0	1.0	1.0	1.0	1.0
Calcium (%)	1.0	0.7	0.65	2.3	0.8	2.5
Chlorine (%)	0.11	0.11	0.11	0.15	0.15	0.15
Phosphorus (%)	0.8	0.6	0.65	1.0	0.65	0.8
Sodium (%)	0.1	0.1	0.085	0.15	0.15	0.15
Iodine (mg)	0.3	0.3	0.30	0.30	0.30	0.30
Magnesium (mg)	600	400	600	400	150	500
Manganese (mg)	90	70	90	70	90	70
Zinc (mg)	60	50	50	50	25	50

[a]The values in lightface type are estimates. For nutrients not listed see requirements for turkeys as a guide.
[b]May be reduced to 20 percent at 6 weeks of age.
[c]May be reduced to 20 percent at 3 weeks of age.

TABLE 7 Nutrient Requirements of Ducks[a] (in Percentage or Amount per Kilogram of Feed)

Nutrient	Starting and Growing Ducks	Breeding Ducks
Metabolizable energy (kcal/kg)	2,900	2,900
Protein (%)	16[b]	15
Lysine (%)	. 0.9	0.7
Methionine + cystine (%)	0.8	0.55
Vitamin A (IU)	4,000	4,000
Vitamin D (ICU)	220	500
Riboflavin (mg)	4	4
Pantothenic acid (mg)	11	10
Niacin (mg)	55	40
Pyridoxine (mg)	2.6	3
Calcium (%)	0.6	2.75
Phosphorus (%)	0.6[c]	0.6
Sodium (%)	0.15	0.15
Manganese (mg)	40	25
Magnesium (mg)	500	500

[a]The values in lightface type are estimates. For nutrients not listed, see requirements for chickens as a guide.
[b]Increasing protein level to 22 percent for the first 2 weeks will increase early growth.
[c]See text page 7.

TABLE 8 Nutrient Requirements of Geese[a] (in Percentage or Amount per Kilogram of Feed)

Nutrient	Starting (0-6 Weeks)	Growing (after 6 Weeks)	Breeding
Metabolizable energy (kcal/kg)	2,900	2,900	2,900
Protein (%)	22	15	15
Lysine (%)	0.9	0.6	0.6
Vitamin A (IU)	1,500	1,500	4,000
Vitamin D (ICU)	200	200	200
Riboflavin (mg)	4	2.5	4
Niacin, available (mg)	55	35	20
Calcium (%)	0.8	0.6	2.25
Phosphorus (%)	0.6	0.4	0.6

[a]The values in lightface type are estimates. For nutrients not listed, see requirements for chickens as a guide.

TABLE 9 Water Consumption[a] by Chickens and Turkeys of Different Ages

Age (Weeks)	1,000 Chicken Broilers/Day		1,000 Egg Strain Pullets/Day		1,000 Turkeys/Day	
	Liters	Gallons	Liters	Gallons	Liters	Gallons
1	23	6[b]	19	5[b]	37	10[b]
2	42	12[b]	38	10[b]	76	20[b]
3	67	17	45	12	113	30
4	126	34	64	17	151	40
5	140	38	83	22	189	50
6	170	47	94	25	227	60
7	207	56	105	28	283	75
8	235	64	113	30	359	95
9			132	35	434	115
10			143	38	473	125
12			151	40	567	150
16			158	42	605	160
20			170	45		
35	Laying or breeding		190	50	♂ 700	185
					♀ 450	119

[a]Will vary considerably depending on temperature (see page 10).
[b]By end of week.

TABLE 10 Vitamins or Minerals Associated with Various Signs of Deficiencies[a]

Deficiency Sign	Description	Species	Associated Vitamin or Mineral
Skin lesions	Crusting and scab formation around eyes and beak	Chick, poult	Pantothenic acid
	Bottoms of feet rough and calloused with hemorrhagic cracks	Chick, poult	Biotin
	Scalines on feet	Chick	Zinc, niacin
	Lesions around eyes, eyelids stuck together	Chick, poult	Vitamin A
	Mouth, inflammation of oral mucosa (chicken black tongue)	Poult, chick	Niacin
Feather abnormalities	Uneven feather growth, abnormally long primary feathers, feathers not lying smoothly	Chick, poult	Protein, amino acid imbalance
	Frizzled and rough	Chick, poult	Zinc, niacin, pantothenic acid
	Black pigmentation in breeds with red or brown feathers	Chick	Vitamin D
	Depigmentation	Turkey	Selenium
Nervous disorders	Convulsion with head retraction	Chick, pigeon	Thiamine
	Convulsions and hyperexcitability	Chick, poult, duckling	Vitamin B$_6$
	Hyperirritability	Chick, poult, duckling	Magnesium
	Characteristic fright reaction with tetanic spasms	Chick	Chloride
	Spastic cervical paralysis, neck extended with birds appearing to look down	Poult	Folacin
	Curled-toe paralysis, gross enlargement of sciatic and brachial nerves with myelin degeneration	Chicks	Riboflavin
	Encephalomalacia, tetanic spasms with head retraction, hemorrhagic lesions in cerebellum	Chicks	Vitamin E

34

		Ducklings	
Blood and vascular system	Anemic		
	Macrocytic		Vitamin B_{12}
	Macrocytic, hyperchromic		Folacin
	Microcytic, hypochromic		Iron, copper
	Macrocytic		Vitamin B_6
	Hemorrhage, internal, intramuscular, subcutaneous internal from aortic rupture, exudative diathesis	Chicks, poult	Selenium, vitamin K, vitamin E
	Enlarged heart	Chicks, poult	Copper
Muscle	Muscular dystrophy, white areas of degeneration in skeletal muscle	Chick, duck, poult	Vitamin E, selenium
	Cardiac myopathy	Poult	Vitamin E, selenium
	Gizzard myopathy	Poult	Vitamin E, selenium
Bone disorders	Soft, easily bent bones and beak (rickets)	All poultry	Vitamin D, calcium or phosphorus deficiency or imbalance
	Hock enlargement	Poult, chick, gosling, duckling	Niacin, zinc
	Perosis	Chick, poult	Biotin, choline, vitamin B_{12}, manganese, zinc, folacin
	Bowed legs	Ducks	Niacin
	Shortening and thickening of leg bones	Chicks	Zinc, manganese
	Curled toes		Riboflavin
Diarrhea		Duck, poult, chick	Niacin, riboflavin, biotin

ªSlow growth and general lack of vigor are generally associated with malnutrition. These signs are more specific indications of deficiencies of particular nutrients.

TABLE 11 Toxic Levels of Inorganic Elements for Poultry (Based on Levels in Feed Unless Otherwise Indicated)

Element	Species	Age	Compound	Toxic Level (ppm)	Physiological Effect	Reference
Aluminum	Chicken	Immature	$AlCl_2$	500	Reduced growth	Storer and Nelson, 1968
Aluminum	Chicken	Immature	$Al_2(SO_4)_3$	1,000	Reduced growth (1.6% Al_2O_3 not toxic)	Storer and Nelson, 1968
Aluminum	Chicken	Immature	$Al_2(SO_4)_3 \cdot 18H_2O$	2,200	Rickets	Deobold and Elvehjem, 1935
Barium	Chicken	Immature	?	200	Reduced growth	Taucins et al., 1969
Barium	Chicken	Immature	?	2,000	Death	Taucins et al., 1969
Bromine	Chicken	Immature	NaBr	5,000	Reduced growth	Doberenz et al., 1965
Cadmium	Chicken	Immature	$CdSO_4$	100	Reduced growth	Hill et al., 1964
Cadmium	Chicken	Immature	$CdSO_4 \cdot H_2O$	25	Reduced growth	Hill et al., 1963
Cadmium	Chicken	Immature	?	100	Reduced growth	Weber and Reid, 1971
Cadmium	Chicken	Immature	$CdSO_4$	40	Reduced growth	Hill, 1974
Cadmium	Turkey	Immature	$CdCl_2$	20	Reduced growth	Supplee et al., 1961
Chlorine	Chicken	Immature	Arginine, NaCl and KCl	15,000	Reduced growth	Nesheim et al., 1964
Chromium	Chicken	Immature	K_2CrO_4	300	Reduced growth	Kuniahia et al., 1966
Chromium	Chicken	Immature	$Cr_2(SO_4)_3$	300	Reduced growth	Kuniahia et al., 1966
Cobalt	Chicken	Immature	$CoCl_2 \cdot 6H_2O$	200	Reduced growth	Hill, 1974
Copper	Chicken	Immature	CuO	806 (practical diet)	Reduced growth; mortality	Mehring et al., 1960
Copper	Chicken	Immature	$CuSO_4$	324 (practical diet)	Reduced growth; muscular dystrophy	Mayo et al., 1956
Copper	Chicken	Immature	$CuSO_4$	1,270 (practical or purified diet)	Mortality	Mayo et al., 1956
Copper	Chicken	Immature	$CuSO_4 \cdot 5H_2O$	500	Reduced growth; gizzard erosion	Poupoulis and Jensen, 1976
Copper	Chicken	Immature	$CuSO_4 \cdot 5H_2O$	800	Exudative diathesis; muscular dystrophy	Jensen, 1975a
Copper	Turkey	Immature	$CuSO_4 \cdot 5H_2O$	676 (practical diet)	Reduced growth	Vohra and Kratzer, 1968
Copper	Turkey	Immature	$CuSO_4 \cdot 5H_2O$	800 (purified diet)	Reduced growth	Supplee, 1964
Copper	Turkey	Immature	$CuCO_3$	50 (purified diet)	Reduced growth	Waibel et al., 1964
Fluorine	Chicken	Immature	NaF	1,000 (practical diet not toxic)	Reduced growth	Doberenz et al., 1965
Fluorine	Chicken	Immature	NaF	500 NaF (similar level of F as CaF_2 not toxic)	Reduced growth	Gardiner et al., 1959
Fluorine	Chicken	Immature	NaF	500	Reduced growth	Weber, 1969
Fluorine	Chicken	Immature	NaF	750	Reduced growth	Berg, 1972
Iodine	Chicken	Laying hen	KI	625	Reduced egg production, egg size, and hatchability	Arrington et al., 1967
Iron	Chicken	Immature	$Fe_2(SO_4)_3$	4,500	Rickets	Deobold and Elvehjem, 1935
Lead	Chicken	Immature	Pb acetate	1,000	Reduced growth	Damron et al., 1969
Magnesium	Chicken	Immature	$MgCO_3$	6,000	Reduced growth	Chicco et al., 1967
Magnesium	Chicken	Immature	$MgCO_3$	6,400	Reduced growth; mortality	Nugara and Edwards, 1963
Manganese	Turkey	Immature	$MnSO_4 \cdot H_2O$	4,800	Reduced growth	Vohra, 1972
Mercury	Chicken	Immature	$HgSO_4$	400	Reduced growth	Hill, 1964
Mercury	Chicken	Immature	$HgCl_2$	250 (water)	Reduced growth; mortality	Parkhurst and Thaxton, 1973
Mercury	Chicken	Immature	$HgCl_2$	400	Reduced growth	Hill et al., 1964
Molybdenum	Chicken	Immature	Na_2MoO_4	200	Reduced growth; mortality	Arthur et al., 1958
Molybdenum	Chicken	Immature	Na_2MoO_4	500	Reduced growth; mortality	Davies et al., 1960
Molybdenum	Chicken	Immature	$Na_2MoO_4 \cdot 2H_2O$	350	Reduced growth	Berg and Martinson, 1972
Molybdenum	Chicken	Laying hen	$Na_2MoO_4 \cdot 2H_2O$	500	Reduced egg production and hatchability	Lepore and Miller, 1965
NaCl	Chicken	Immature	NaCl	7,000#	Reduced growth; mortality	Krista et al., 1961

36

Element	Species	Age	Compound	Level	Effect	Reference
NaCl	Chicken	Laying hen	NaCl	10,000[a]	Reduced egg production	Krista et al., 1961
NaCl	Turkey	Immature	NaCl	4,000[a]	Reduced body weight; mortality	Krista et al., 1961
NaCl	Duck	Immature	NaCl	4,000[a]	Reduced body weight	Krista et al., 1961
NaCl	Turkey	Mature	NaCl	60,000	Reduced growth	Roberts, 1957
NaCl	Turkey	Immature	NaCl	40,000	Reduced growth; pendulous crop	Harper and Arscott, 1962
Nickel	Chicken	Immature	$NiSO_4$ or Ni-acetate	500	Reduced growth	Weber and Reid, 1968
Nitrate	Turkey	Immature	$NaNO_3$	900[a]	Reduced growth; mortality	Adams et al., 1967
Nitrate	Turkey	Immature	$NaNO_3$	450 (N)[a]	No effect on meat color	Mugler et al., 1970
Nitrite	Chicken	Immature	$NaNO_2$	365 (N)[a]	Decreased vitamin A in liver and thyroid	Sell and Roberts, 1967
Selenium	Chicken	Immature	Na_2SeO_3 + Se wheat	10	Reduced growth	Carlson and Lellis, 1957
Selenium	Chicken	Immature	Na_2SeO_3	10	Reduced growth	Jensen, 1975b
Selenium	Chicken	Immature	Na_2SeO_3	20 (with 1,000 Ca)	Reduced growth	Jensen, 1975b
Selenium	Chicken	Immature	Na_2SeO_3	40 (with 1,000 Ag)	None	Jensen, 1975b
Selenium	Chicken	Laying hen	Seleniferous wheat	10	Reduced hatchability	Moxon and Wilson, 1944
Silver	Chicken	Immature	$AgSO_4$	200	Reduced growth	Hill, 1964
Silver	Chicken	Immature	$AgNO_3$	900	Exudative diathesis (prevented by Se or vitamin E)	Peterson and Jensen, 1975a
Silver	Chicken	Immature	$AgNO_3$	900	Anemia, enlarged hearts, and muscular diathesis (prevented by Cu)	Peterson and Jensen, 1975b
Silver	Turkey	Immature	Ag acetate or nitrate	900	Anemia, enlarged hearts, and muscular dystrophy (prevented by Cu + Se)	Jensen et al., 1974
Sodium	Chicken	Immature	Na glutamate	8,900[b]	Reduced growth	Nesheim et al., 1964
Sodium	Chicken	Laying hen	Na_2SO_4	12,000[a]	Reduced egg production	Krista et al., 1964
Strontium	Chicken	Immature	$SrCO_3$	6,000	Reduced growth	Weber et al., 1968
Sulfate	Chicken	Immature	$CaSO_4$	26,000	Reduced growth	Nesheim et al., 1964
Sulfate	Chicken	Laying hen	SO_4	2,700 (S)	Reduced egg production	Krista et al., 1964
Vanadium	Chicken	Immature	?	20	Reduced growth	Berg, 1966
Vanadium	Chicken	Immature	$Ca_3(VO_4)_2$	30	Reduced growth	Romoser et al., 1961
Vanadium	Chicken	Immature	$Ca_3(VO_4)_2$	200	Mortality	Romoser et al., 1964
Vanadium	Chicken	Immature	NH_4VO_3 or $VOSO_4$	25	Reduced growth; mortality	Hathcock et al., 1964
Vanadium	Chicken	Immature	$NaVO_3$	5	Reduced growth	Hill, 1974
Vanadium	Chicken	Laying hen	NH_4VO_3	15	Depressed albumin quality; reduced growth	Berg, 1963
Vanadium	Chicken	Laying hen	NH_4VO_3	20	Depressed albumin quality; reduced body weight	Berg, 1963
Vanadium	Chicken	Laying hen	NH_4VO_3	30	Depressed egg production	Berg, 1963
Vanadium	Chicken	Laying hen	NH_4VO_3	50	Depressed hatchability	Berg, 1963
Vanadium	Chicken	Immature	$Na_4V_2O_7$	10	Reduced growth	Berg, 1963
Zinc	Chicken	Immature	$ZnSO_4$	1,500	Reduced growth	Roberson and Schaible, 1960
Zinc	Chicken	Immature	$ZnCO_3$	1,500	Reduced growth	Roberson and Schaible, 1960
Zinc	Chicken	Immature	ZnO	3,000	Reduced growth	Johnson et al., 1962
Zinc	Chicken	Immature	ZnO	2,000	Toxicity	Berg, 1972
Zinc	Chicken	Immature	ZnO	800	Reduced growth and bone ash (sucrose-fish meal diet)	Berg, 1972
Zinc	Chicken	Immature	$ZnSO_4$	2,000	Exudative diathesis; muscular dystrophy (0.5 ppm Se in diet)	Jensen, 1975a
Zinc	Chicken	Immature	$ZnSO_4$	3,000	Reduced growth (0.5 ppm Se in diet)	Jensen, 1975a

[a] In water.
[b] Diet low in Cl⁻ ion.

TABLE 12 Daily Nutrient Requirements per Female (Single-Comb White Leghorns and Similar Breeds)

Nutrient	Body Weight (g) of Growing Chicken						Body Weight (g) of Mature Hen		
							Mainte-nance	Laying[a]	Breeding[a]
	250	500	750	1,000	1,250	1,500	1,800	1,800	1,800
Total daily feed (g)	21	43	52	60	71	78	70	110	110
Crude protein (g)	3.8	6.4	7.8	9.0	8.5	9.4	?	16.5	16.5
Methionine (g)	0.07	0.12	0.14	0.16	0.15	0.16	?	0.30	0.30
Methionine and cystine (g)	0.12	0.22	0.26	0.30	0.28	0.31	?	0.55	0.55
Lysine (g)	0.18	0.26	0.31	0.36	0.32	0.35	?	0.66	0.66
Calcium (g)	0.19	0.36	0.31	0.36	0.43	0.47	?	3.6	3.0
Phosphorus (g)	0.15	0.30	0.21	0.24	0.28	0.31	?	0.55	0.55
Sodium (g)	0.03	0.07	0.08	0.09	0.11	0.12	?	0.16	0.16
Potassium (g)	0.04	0.09	0.08	0.10	0.11	0.13	?	0.11	0.11
Magnesium (mg)	12.6	25.8	20.8	24.0	28.4	31.2	?	55	55
Manganese (mg)	1.2	2.4	1.3	1.5	1.8	2.0	?	2.75	3.6
Iodine (mg)	0.01	0.02	0.02	0.02	0.03	0.03	?	0.03	0.03
Vitamin A (IU)	32	65	78	90	106	117	?	440	440
Vitamin D (ICU)	4.2	8.6	10.4	12.0	14.2	15.6	?	55	55
Thiamine (mg)	0.04	0.08	0.07	0.08	0.09	0.10	?	?	0.09
Riboflavin (mg)	0.08	0.16	0.10	0.11	0.13	0.14	?	0.24	0.42
Pantothenic acid (mg)	0.21	0.43	0.52	0.60	0.71	0.78	?	0.24	1.10
Niacin (mg)	0.57	1.16	0.57	0.66	0.78	0.86	?	1.1	1.1
Pyridoxine (mg)	0.06	0.13	0.16	0.18	0.21	0.23	?	0.33	0.49
Biotin (mg)	0.003	0.006	0.005	0.006	0.007	0.008	?	?	0.024
Choline (mg)	27	56	26	30	36	39	?	?	?
Folacin (mg)	0.012	0.024	0.013	0.015	0.017	0.020	?	0.03	0.04
Vitamin B_{12} (mg)	0.0002	0.0004	0.0002	0.0002	0.0002	0.0002	?	?	0.0003
Approximate age (weeks)	4	7	11	14	17	21	—	—	—

[a]Sixty-five percent production.

TABLE 13 Daily Nutrient Requirements per Chicken (Chickens of Broiler Strains)

| Nutrient | Body Weight (g) of Growing Animal | | | | | | Body Weight (g) of Mature Animal | | |
| | | | | | | | Mainte-nance | Laying[a] | Breeding[a] |
	250	500	750	1,000	1,500	2,000	2,500	2,500	2,500
Total daily feed (g)	28	51	73	98	113	120	87	135	135
Crude protein (g)	6	12	15	20	20	22	?	20	20
Methionine (g)	0.14	0.25	0.28	0.37	0.36	0.38	?	0.36	0.36
Methionine and cystine (g)	0.26	0.47	0.53	0.70	0.68	0.72	?	0.68	0.68
Lysine (g)	0.34	0.61	0.73	0.98	0.96	1.02	?	0.81	0.81
Calcium (g)	0.25	0.46	0.66	0.87	1.01	0.71	?	4.4	3.7
Phosphorus (g)	0.19	0.36	0.51	0.68	0.79	0.48	?	0.68	0.68
Sodium (g)	0.04	0.07	0.11	0.14	0.19	0.18	?	0.20	0.20
Potassium (g)	0.06	0.10	0.14	0.19	0.23	0.20	?	0.13	0.13
Magnesium (mg)	17	31	44	59	67	48	?	68	68
Manganese (mg)	1.5	2.8	4.0	5.4	6.1	3.0	?	3.4	4.4
Iodine (mg)	0.01	0.02	0.02	0.03	0.04	0.04	?	0.04	0.04
Vitamin A (IU)	42	76	110	150	170	180	?	540	540
Vitamin D (ICU)	5.6	10	15	20	23	24	?	68	68
Thiamine (mg)	0.05	0.09	0.13	0.18	0.20	0.16	?	?	0.11
Riboflavin (mg)	0.10	0.18	0.26	0.36	0.41	0.22	?	0.30	0.51
Pantothenic acid (mg)	0.28	0.51	0.73	0.98	1.13	1.20	?	0.30	1.35
Niacin (mg)	0.62	1.37	1.97	2.64	3.08	1.30	?	1.35	1.35
Pyridoxine (mg)	0.08	0.15	0.22	0.29	0.34	0.36	?	0.40	0.40
Biotin (mg)	0.004	0.008	0.011	0.014	0.017	0.012	?	?	0.024
Choline (mg)	41	66	95	129	128	80	?	?	?
Folacin (mg)	0.015	0.028	0.040	0.054	0.061	0.03	?	0.03	0.05
Vitamin B$_{12}$ (mg)	0.0003	0.0005	0.0007	0.0009	0.0010	0.0004	?	?	0.0004
Approximate age (weeks) ♂ + ♀	2.1	3.2	4.3	5.3	6.6	8.2	—	—	—

[a]Sixty percent production.

TABLE 14 Feed Required per Day by Adult Chickens in Relation to Body Weight and Egg Production[a]

Body Weight (kg)	Feed Required (g/Hen/Day) at Percent Production:					
	0	50	60	70	80	90
1.00	42	72	77	83	89	96
1.25	49	78	87	90	96	104
1.50	56	85	91	96	103	110
1.75	62	91	96	103	108	114
2.00	67	96	102	108	113	120
2.25	73	102	107	113	119	125
2.50	78	107	112	119	124	130
2.75	83	112	118	123	130	135
3.00	88	117	122	129	134	140
3.25	93	121	127	133	139	145
3.50	97	126	131	138	143	149
3.75	101	131	136	142	148	154
4.00	106	135	140	147	152	158

[a]Based on the following equation developed by Byerly (1941):

$$F = 0.523\,W^{0.663} \pm 1.126\,\Delta W + 1.135\,E$$

where

F = feed consumption in grams per hen per day
W = average body weight in grams
ΔW = average daily change in body weight in grams (assumed 0) average
E = grams of egg produced per hen per day

Assume 21.1°C (70°F). For each 1°C increase in temperature, feed consumption is expected to decrease about 1.2 percent (about 0.67 percent per 1°F).

TABLE 15 Body Weights and Feed Requirements for Meat-Type and Egg-Type Chickens and Capons[a]

Age (Weeks)	Body Weights (g)				Cumulative Feed Consumption (g)			
	Leghorn[b]		Broiler[c]		Leghorn		Broiler	
	♂	♀	♂	♀	♂	♀	♂	♀
2	130	130	250	240	360	360	265	250
4	270	250	740	650	725	725	1,110	975
6	450	430	1,340	1,190	1,400	1,350	2,425	2,175
8	690	540	2,100	1,760	2,400	1,900	4,200	3,600
10	940	725	2,720	1,990	3,400	2,750	6,250	4,750
12	1,240	880	3,240	2,370	4,900	3,800	8,125	6,350
14	1,350	1,010	3,640	2,650	5,500	4,300	11,150	8,100
16	1,450	1,155	3,990	2,880	6,200	5,100	13,650	10,225
18	1,550	1,315	4,280	3,060	7,200	6,300	16,650	12,350
20	1,700	1,450	4,540	3,230	8,800	7,600	19,575	14,890

[a]Capons will follow closely the male except immediately following surgery.
[b]Egg strains (Leghorn types) are frequently restricted in the growing period.
[c]Broiler breeders are normally restricted to below these weights by reduced light and feed. Birds to be sold at broiler weights are fed for near maximum rates of gain.

TABLE 16 Growth Rate and Feed Consumption of
Large-Type Turkeys

Age (Weeks)	Body Weight (kg)		Feed Consumption by 2-Week Periods (kg)		Cumulative Feed Consumption (kg)	
	♂	♀	♂	♀	♂	♀
2	0.3	0.2	0.3	0.2	0.3	0.2
4	0.8	0.6	0.8	0.7	1.1	0.9
6	1.7	1.5	1.7	1.6	2.8	2.5
8	2.9	2.5	2.1	1.9	4.9	4.4
10	4.3	3.4	2.9	2.8	7.8	7.2
12	5.7	4.4	3.6	2.5	11.4	9.7
14	7.0	5.3	4.7	3.1	16.1	12.8
16	8.3	5.9	4.6	3.3	20.7	16.1
18	9.7	6.6	6.4	3.6	27.1	19.7
20	11.0	7.2	6.0	3.3	33.1	23.0
22	12.3	7.6	5.2	3.7	38.3	26.7
24	13.7	8.0	6.8	3.0	45.1	29.7
26	14.9	--	8.5	--	53.6	--
28	16.0	--	10.5	--	64.1	--

TABLE 17 Growth Rate and Feed Consumption of Ducks

Age (Weeks)	Body Weight (kg)		Feed Consumption by 1-Week Periods (kg)		Cumulative Feed Consumption (kg)	
	♂	♀	♂	♀	♂	♀
0	0.05	0.05	--	--	--	--
1	0.27	0.27	0.22	0.22	0.22	0.22
2	0.78	0.74	0.77	0.73	0.99	0.95
3	1.38	1.28	1.12	1.11	2.11	2.05
4	1.96	1.82	1.28	1.28	3.40	3.33
5	2.49	2.30	1.48	1.43	4.87	4.76
6	2.96	2.73	1.63	1.59	6.50	6.35
7	3.34	3.06	1.68	1.63	8.18	7.98
8	3.61	3.29	1.68	1.63	9.86	9.61

TABLE 18   Average Composition of Some Commonly Used Feeds for Poultry (Excluding Amino Acids)[a]

Line No.	Feedstuff	International Feed No.	Dry Matter (%)	Energy (kcal/kg) ME_n	Pro	Protein (%)	Ether Extract (%)	Crude Fiber (%)	Calcium (%)	Phosphorus (%)	Potassium (%)	Chlorine (%)	Iron (%)	Magnesium (%)
	Alfalfa meal, dehydrated													
01	17% Protein	1-00-023	92	1,370	580	17.5	2.0	24.1	1.44	0.22	2.17	0.48	0.048	0.36
02	20% Protein	1-00-024	92	1,630	850	20.0	3.8	20.2	1.67	0.28	2.21	0.46	0.039	0.36
03	Barley	4-00-549	89	2,640	1,790	11.6	1.8	5.1	0.03	0.36	0.48	0.15	0.005	0.14
04	Barley, Pacific coast	4-07-939	89	2,620	1,720	9.0	2.0	6.4	0.05	0.32	0.53	0.15	0.011	0.12
05	Blood meal, vat dried	5-00-380	94	2,830	2,280	81.1	1.6	0.5	0.55	0.42	0.09	0.27	0.202	0.16
	Blood meal, spray or ring dried													
06		5-00-381	93	3,420	2,280	88.9	1.0	0.6	0.08	0.09	0.41	0.27	0.30	0.40
07	Bone meal, steamed	6-00-400	97	1,090	—	12.6	—	4.8	29.39	12.58	0.09	0.01	0.32	0.11
08	Brewer's dried grains	5-02-141	92	2,080	1,850	25.3	6.2	15.3	0.29	0.52	0.09	0.12	0.025	0.16
09	Buckwheat	4-00-994	88	2,660	1,800	10.8	2.5	10.5	0.09	0.32	0.40	0.04	—	0.09
10	Buttermilk, dried	5-01-160	92	2,770	1,720	31.6	5.0	0.4	1.32	0.93	0.85	0.47	0.001	0.40
11	Casein, dried	5-01-162	93	4,130	2,500	87.2	0.8	0.2	0.61	1.0	—	—	—	—
12	Corn, yellow	4-02-935	89	3,430	2,520	8.8	3.8	2.2	0.02	0.28	0.30	0.04	0.035	0.12
13	Corn, ground ear	4-02-849	85	2,770	1,980	7.8	3.0	8.7	0.04	0.21	0.45	0.04	0.007	0.13
	Corn													
14	Gluten feed	5-02-903	90	1,750	1,120	22.0	2.5	8.0	0.4	0.8	0.57	0.22	0.046	0.29
15	Gluten meal, 41%	5-02-900	91	2,940	1,850	41.0	2.5	7.0	0.23	0.55	0.30	0.11	0.040	0.05
16	Gluten meal, 60%	5-09-318	90	3,720	2,820	62.0	2.5	1.3	—	0.50	0.35	0.05	0.040	0.15
	Cottonseed meal, expeller													
17		5-01-617	93	2,320	1,520	40.9	3.9	10.8	0.20	1.05	1.19	0.04	0.016	0.52
18	Cottonseed meal, solvent	5-07-872	90	2,400	1,320	41.4	0.5	13.6	0.15	0.97	1.22	0.03	0.011	0.40
	Distiller's dried grains w/solubles (corn)													
19		5-02-843	93	2,480	1,960	27.2	9.0	9.1	0.17	0.72	0.65	0.17	0.028	0.19
	Distiller's dried solubles (corn)													
20		5-02-844	92	2,930	2,240	28.5	9.0	4.0	0.35	1.33	1.75	0.26	0.056	0.64
21	Feather meal, hydrolyzed	5-03-795	93	2,360	1,320	86.4	3.3	1.0	0.33	0.55	0.31	—	—	0.20
22	Fish meal, anchovy	5-01-985	92	2,580	1,890	64.2	5.0	1.0	3.73	2.43	0.69	0.29	0.022	0.24
23	Fish meal, herring	5-02-000	93	3,190	2,050	72.3	10.0	0.7	2.29	1.70	1.09	0.90	0.014	0.15
24	Fish meal, menhaden	5-02-009	92	2,820	1,980	60.5	9.4	0.7	5.11	2.88	0.77	0.60	0.044	0.16
25	Fish meal, sardine	5-02-015	92	2,880	1,980	64.7	5.4	1.0	4.38	2.58	0.25	0.41	0.030	0.10
26	Fish meal, white	5-02-025	95	2,570	1,815	60.9	3.4	—	5.40	2.60	1.0	0.52	0.008	0.22
27	Fish solubles, condensed	5-01-969	51	1,460	990	31.5	7.8	0.2	0.30	0.76	1.74	2.65	0.016	0.02
28	Fish solubles, dried	5-01-971	92	2,830	1,610	63.6	9.3	0.5	1.23	1.63	0.37	—	0.030	0.30
29	Gelatin	5-14-503	91	2,360	1,770	88.0	trace	—	0.50	trace	—	—	—	0.05
30	Hominy feed	4-02-887	90	2,970	1,890	10.0	6.9	6.0	0.04	0.50	0.46	0.05	0.007	0.16
31	Limestone, ground	6-02-632	98	—	—	—	—	—	36.23	0.02	0.12	0.03	0.341	2.01
32	Liver meal	5-00-389	92	2,860	2,400	65.6	15.0	1.4	0.56	1.25	—	—	0.063	—
33	Meat and bone meal	5-00-388	93	1,960	1,600	50.4	8.6	2.8	10.1	4.96	1.02	0.74	0.049	1.12
34	Meat meal	5-00-385	92	2,000	1,870	54.4	7.1	8.7	8.27	4.10	0.6	0.91	0.044	0.58
35	Molasses, beet	4-00-668	79	1,990	1,560	6.1	—	—	0.13	0.06	4.83	1.30	0.007	0.23
36	Molasses, cane, dried	4-04-696	91	1,960	1,540	7.8	0.5	3.3	1.10	0.12	2.60	—	0.095	0.33
37	Oats	4-03-309	89	2,550	1,810	11.4	4.2	10.8	0.06	0.27	0.45	0.11	0.007	0.16
38	Oats, West Coast	4-07-999	91	2,610	1,780	9.0	—	11.0	0.08	0.30	0.37	0.12	—	—
39	Oat hulls	1-03-281	92	400	220	4.6	1.4	28.7	0.13	0.10	0.53	0.10	0.010	—
40	Oyster shell	6-03-481	95	40	—	0.9	—	—	37.26	0.07	0.09	0.01	0.272	0.28
41	Pea, seed	5-03-600	90	2,570	—	23.8	1.3	5.5	0.11	0.42	1.02	0.06	0.005	0.13
42	Peanut meal, expeller	5-03-649	90	2,500	1,870	39.8	7.3	13.0	0.16	0.56	1.13	0.03	—	0.33
43	Peanut meal, solvent	5-03-650	92	2,200	1,900	50.7	1.2	11.9	0.20	0.63	1.19	0.03	—	0.04
44	Poultry by-product meal	5-03-798	93	2,670	1,980	60.5	13.0	2.0	3.0	1.7	0.30	0.54	0.044	0.22
45	Rapeseed meal, expeller	5-03-870	94	2,040	—	35.0	8.6	12.4	0.72	1.09	0.8	—	0.018	0.51
46	Rice bran	4-03-928	91	1,630	1,540	12.9	13.0	11.4	0.07	1.50	1.73	0.07	0.019	0.95
47	Rice, broken	4-03-932	89	2,990	2,510	8.7	—	9.8	0.08	0.39	0	0.08	—	0.11
48	Rice, polishing	4-03-943	90	3,090	2,090	12.2	11.0	4.1	0.05	1.31	1.06	0.11	0.016	0.65
49	Safflower meal, solvent	5-04-110	91	1,600	1,160	42.5	1.3	15.0	0.4	1.3	0.67	0.03	0.048	0.26
50	Sesame meal, expeller	5-04-220	93	2,210	1,720	43.8	8.6	9.7	1.99	1.37	1.20	0.06	—	0.77
51	Skim milk, dried	5-01-175	93	2,520	1,670	33.5	0.9	0.2	1.28	1.02	1.59	0.50	0.001	0.11
52	Sorghum, grain (milo)	4-04-444	89	3,370	2,400	8.9	2.8	2.3	0.03	0.28	0.32	0.09	0.004	0.13

Line No.	Man-ganese (mg/kg)	So-dium (%)	Sul-fur (%)	Copper (mg/kg)	Sele-nium (mg/kg)	Zinc (mg/kg)	Biotin (mg/kg)	Choline (mg/kg)	Folacin (mg/kg)	Niacin (mg/kg)	Panto-thenic acid (mg/kg)	Pyri-doxine (mg/kg)	Ribo-flavin (mg/kg)	This-mine (mg/kg)	Vitamin B_{12} (mg/kg)	Vitamin E (mg/kg)
01	30.0	0.12	0.17	10.2	0.338	24	0.30	1,401	4.2	38	25	6.5	13.6	3.4	0.004	125
02	42.3	0.13	0.43	11.2	0.288	25	0.33	1,419	3.3	40	34	8.0	15.2	5.8	0.004	144
03	–	0.04	0.15	10.2	0.10	17	0.15	990	0.7	55	8	3.0	1.8	1.9	–	20
04	16.3	0.02	0.15	7.7	0.102	15	0.15	1,034	0.5	48	7	–	1.6	4.0	–	20
05	5.1	0.32	0.32	9.7	0.01	–	0.08	695	0.1	29	3	–	2.6	0.4	44.0	–
06	6.4	0.33	0.32	8.1	–	306	0.20	280	0.4	13	5	4.4	1.3	0.5	44.0	–
07	40.9	0.07	0.32	8.3	–	425	–	693	–	30	3	–	5.9	0.4	0.069	–
08	37.8	0.15	0.31	21.1	0.70	98	0.96	1,723	7.1	29	8	0.65	1.4	0.5	–	25
09	33.8	0.05	–	9.5	–	9	–	440	–	19	12	–	5.5	4.0	–	–
10	3.4	0.73	0.03	–	–	–	0.29	1,707	0.4	9	34	2.43	31.3	3.3	0.037	6
11	4.2	–	–	4.0	–	–	0.05	205	0.5	1	3	0.4	1.5	0.5	–	–
12	5.0	0.02	0.08	3.2	0.03	10	0.06	620	0.4	24	4	7.0	1.0	3.5	–	22
13	7.7	0.01	0.18	6.7	0.073	9	0.05	393	0.3	17	4	5.0	0.9	–	–	19
14	23.8	0.95	0.22	47.9	0.1	7	0.33	1,518	0.3	66	17	15.0	2.4	2.0	–	15
15	8.9	0.07	0.40	28.3	1.0	20	0.18	926	0.4	50	10	7.9	1.7	0.2	–	20
16	4.4	0.02	0.43	26.4	1.0	33	0.15	330	0.2	55	3	6.2	2.2	0.3	–	24
17	22.9	0.04	0.40	18.6	0.06	–	0.60	2,753	1.0	38	10	5.3	5.1	6.4	–	39
18	20.0	0.04	–	17.8	–	82	0.55	2,933	2.7	40	7	3.0	4.0	3.3	–	–
19	23.9	0.48	0.30	56.6	0.390	80	0.78	2,637	0.9	71	11	2.20	8.6	2.9	–	40
20	73.7	0.26	0.37	82.7	0.332	85	1.10	4,842	1.1	116	21	10	17.0	6.9	–	55
21	21.0	0.71	–	–	–	54	0.44	891	0.2	27	10	–	2.1	0.1	0.078	–
22	9.5	0.88	0.54	9.3	1.363	103	0.23	4,408	0.2	100	15	4.0	7.1	0.1	0.352	4
23	4.7	0.61	0.69	5.9	1.930	132	0.31	5,306	0.8	93	17	4.0	9.9	0.1	0.403	22
24	33.0	0.41	0.45	10.8	2.103	147	0.20	3,056	0.6	55	9	4.0	4.9	0.5	0.104	7
25	23.0	0.18	0.30	20.0	1.756	–	0.10	3,135	–	70	10	–	6.0	0.3	0.235	–
26	9.8	1.1	0.50	6.4	1.714	64	0.12	5,180	0.3	49	10	4.1	6.0	2.1	0.081	8
27	14.4	2.62	0.12	44.9	2.0	38	0.18	3,519	–	169	35	12.2	14.6	5.5	0.347	–
28	50.1	0.37	0.40	–	–	76	0.26	5,507	–	271	55	–	7.7	–	0.401	6
29	–	–	–	–	–	–	–	–	–	–	–	–	–	–	–	–
30	14.5	0.10	0.03	13.3	0.10	3.0	0.13	971	0.3	46	8	11.0	2.2	7.9	–	–
31	247.5	0.06	0.04	–	–	–	–	–	–	–	–	–	–	–	–	–
32	8.8	–	–	88.9	–	–	0.02	11,311	5.5	204	29	–	46.3	0.2	0.498	–
33	14.2	0.72	0.50	1.5	0.25	93	0.64	1,996	0.32	46	4.1	12.8	4.4	0.8	0.070	1.0
34	9.7	1.15	0.49	9.8	0.42	103	0.17	2,077	0.3	57	5	3.0	5.5	0.2	0.068	1.0
35	4.7	0.93	0.48	17.7	–	14	–	829	–	42	4.0	–	2.1	–	–	5.1
36	42.0	0.16	0.35	0.6	–	30	–	891	0.1	43	4	–	2.4	–	–	5.4
37	43.2	0.08	0.21	8.3	0.30	17	0.11	946	0.3	12		1.0	1.1	6.0	–	20.0
38	38.0	–	–	–	0.07	–	0.11	959	0.3	14	13	1.3	1.1	–	–	20.0
39	13.6	0.04	–	3.1	–	0.1	–	284	0.96	7	3	–	1.5	0.6	–	–
40	127.5	0.20	–	–	–	–	–	–	–	–	–	–	–	–	–	–
41	–	0.04	–	–	–	30	0.18	642	0.4	34	10	1.0	2.3	7.5	–	–
42	25.1	0.07	0.29	–	0.28	20	0.76	1,655	0.4	166	47	10.0	5.2	7.1	–	2.9
43	28.9	0.07	–	–	–	20	0.39	2,396	0.4	170	53	10.0	11.0	–	–	3.0
44	11.0	0.40	0.51	14.0	0.75	120	0.30	5,952	1.0	40	12.3	–	11.0	1.0	0.31	2.0
45	61.0	0.5	–	7.0	0.98	44	–	6,464	–	153	9	7.0	3.7	1.7	–	19.1
46	324.5	0.07	0.18	13.0	–	30	0.42	1,135	–	293	23	14.0	2.5	22.5	–	59.8
47	18.0	0.07	0.06	–	–	17	0.08	800	0.2	46	8	–	0.7	–	–	14.5
48	–	0.10	0.17	–	–	26	0.61	1,237	0.2	520	47	–	1.8	19.8	–	90.0
49	15.6	0.10	0.06	8.5	–	33	1.40	2,067	0.4	22	40	–	2.4	–	–	0.7
50	47.0	0.04	0.43	–	–	100	0.34	1,536	–	30	6	12.5	3.6	2.8	–	–
51	2.0	0.44	0.31	11.5	0.12	40	0.33	1,393	0.5	11	37	3.9	19.0	3.5	0.037	9.1
52	13.6	0.04	0.16	19.0	–	14	0.18	450	0.2	41	12	3.2	1.1	4.0	–	12.0

TABLE 18   Average Composition of Some Commonly Used Feeds for Poultry (Excluding Amino Acids)[a]—Continued

Line No.		Man-ganese (mg/kg)	So-dium (%)	Sul-fur (%)	Copper (mg/kg)	Sele-nium (mg/kg)	Zinc (mg/kg)	Biotin (mg/kg)	Choline (mg/kg)	Folacin (mg/kg)	Niacin (mg/kg)	Panto-thenic acid (mg/kg)	Pyri-doxine (mg/kg)	Ribo-flavin (mg/kg)	Thia-mine (mg/kg)	Vitamin B_{12} (mg/kg)	Vitamin E (mg/kg)
53	Soybeans, heat processed				5-04-597	90	3,300	2,170	37.0	18.0	5.5	0.25	0.58	1.61	0.03	0.008	0.28
54	Soybean meal, dehulled				5-04-612	90	2,440	1,730	48.5	1.0	3.9	0.27	0.62	2.02	0.05	–	–
55	Soybean meal, expeller				5-04-600	90	2,430	1,720	42.6	4.0	6.2	0.27	0.61	1.83	0.07	0.014	0.26
56	Soybean meal, solvent				5-04-604	89	2,230	1,570	44.0	0.8	7.3	0.29	0.65	2.00	0.05	0.012	0.27
57	Soybean mill feed				5-04-594	89	720	440	13.3	1.6	33.0	0.37	0.19	1.50	–	–	0.12
58	Soybean protein, isolated[b]				5-08-038	93	3,500	2,300	84.1	0.4	0.2	0.02	0.8	0.18	0.02	0.013	0.013
59	Sunflower meal, solvent dehulled				5-04-739	93	2,320	1,430	45.4	2.9	12.2	0.37	1.0	1.00	0.10	0.003	0.75
60	Wheat bran				4-05-190	90	1,300	1,050	15.7	3.0	11.0	0.14	1.15	1.19	0.06	0.017	0.52
61	Wheat, hard				4-05-268	87	2,800	2,250	14.1	1.9	2.4	0.05	0.37	0.45	0.05	0.005	0.17
62	Wheat middlings				4-05-205	88	1,800	1,130	16.0	3.0	7.5	0.12	0.90	0.99	0.03	0.004	0.16
63	Wheat, soft				4-05-337	89	3,120	1,980	10.2	1.8	2.4	0.05	0.31	0.40	0.08	0.004	0.10
64	Whey, dried				4-01-182	93	1,900	1,540	12.0	0.8	0.2	0.97	0.76	1.05	0.07	0.013	0.13
65	Whey, low lactose				4-01-186	91	2,090	1,580	15.5	1.0	0.3	1.95	0.98	3.0	2.10	–	0.25
66	Yeast, brewer's, dried				7-05-527	93	1,990	1,260	44.4	1.0	2.7	0.12	1.40	1.70	0.12	0.012	0.23
67	Yeast, torula, dried				7-05-534	93	2,160	1,540	47.2	2.5	2.4	0.58	1.67	1.88	0.02	0.009	0.13

[a] As-fed basis
[b] Soybean protein concentrate (AAFCO).

Line No.	Feedstuff			Inter-national Feed No.	Dry Matter (%)	Energy (kcal/kg)		Pro-tein (%)	Ether Extract (%)	Crude Fiber (%)	Cal-cium (%)	Phos-phorus (%)	Potas-sium (%)	Chlo-rine (%)	Iron (%)	Mag-nesium (%)
						ME$_n$	Pro									
53	29.8	0.12	0.22	15.8	0.11	16	0.27	2,860	4.2	22	11	10.8	2.6	11.0	—	40.0
54	43.0	0.25	—	15.0	0.10	45	0.32	2,731	3.6	22	15	5.0	2.9	3.2	—	3.3
55	30.7	0.27	0.33	24.3	0.10	60	0.33	2,703	4.4	32	14	—	3.7	3.2	—	6.1
56	29.3	0.26	0.43	21.5	0.10	27	0.32	2,794	1.3	29	16	—	2.9	4.5	—	2.1
57	28.5	—	0.06	—	—	—	—	640	—	24	13	—	3.5	—	—	—
58	1.0	0.07	0.71	7.0	0.1	23	0.3	2	2.5	6	4.2	5.4	1.2	0.2	—	—
59	22.9	2.0	—	3.5	—	—	1.45	2,894	—	220	24	16.0	4.7	—	—	11.0
60	113.2	0.05	0.22	14.1	0.85	133	0.48	1,880	1.2	186	31	7.0	4.6	8.0	—	13.5
61	31.8	0.04	0.12	5.8	0.2	31	0.11	1,090	0.35	48	9.9	3.4	1.4	4.5	—	12.6
62	118.0	0.12	0.26	18.1	0.8	150	0.37	1,439	0.8	98	13	9.0	2.2	16.5	—	40.5
63	23.8	0.04	0.12	6.9	0.06	28	0.11	1,002	0.4	57	11	4.0	1.2	4.3	—	13.2
64	6.1	0.48	1.04	46.0	0.08	3	0.34	1,369	0.8	10	44	4.0	27.1	4.1	0.023	0.2
65	—	1.50	—	—	0.10	—	0.64	4,392	1.4	18.6	69	3.96	45.8	5.7	0.023	—
66	5.2	0.07	0.38	32.8	1.0	39	1.05	3,984	9.9	448	109	42.8	37.0	91.8	—	—
67	12.8	0.01	0.34	13.5	1.0	99	1.39	2,881	22.4	500	73	—	47.7	6.2	—	—

TABLE 19 Average Amino Acid Composition of Some Commonly Used Feedstuffs[a]

Line No.	Feedstuff	International Feed No.	Dry Matter (%)	Pro-tein (%)	Argi-nine (%)	Gly-cine (%)	Serine (%)	Histi-dine (%)	Iso-leucine (%)	Leu-cine (%)	Ly-sine (%)	Methi-onine (%)	Cys-tine (%)	Phenyl-alanine (%)	Tyro-sine (%)	Thre-onine (%)	Tryp-tophan (%)	Valine (%)
	Alfalfa meal, dehydrated																	
01	17% Protein	1-00-023	92	17.5	0.80	0.90	0.77	0.32	0.84	1.26	0.73	0.23	0.20	0.79	0.56	0.70	0.28	0.84
02	20% Protein	1-00-024	92	20.0	0.92	0.97	0.89	0.34	0.88	1.30	0.87	0.31	0.25	0.85	0.59	0.76	0.33	0.97
03	Barley	4-00-549	89	11.6	0.59	0.40	0.42	0.29	0.49	0.80	0.40	0.17	0.19	0.64	0.33	0.42	0.14	0.62
04	Barley, Pacific coast	4-07-939	89	9.0	0.48	0.36	0.32	0.21	0.40	0.80	0.29	0.13	0.18	0.48	–	0.30	0.12	0.46
05	Blood meal, vat dried	5-00-380	94	81.1	3.63	4.59	3.14	3.52	0.95	10.53	7.06	0.55	0.52	5.66	2.07	3.16	1.29	7.28
06	Blood meal, spray or ring dried	5-00-381	93	88.9	3.81	4.00	3.86	5.26	0.88	11.82	8.86	0.75	0.86	6.55	2.49	3.94	1.34	8.60
07	Bone meal, steamed	6-00-400	97	12.6	1.89	2.65	0.48	0.20	0.49	1.03	0.94	0.19	–	0.60	0.06	0.62	0.05	0.76
08	Brewer's dried grains	5-02-141	92	25.3	1.28	1.09	0.80	0.57	1.44	2.48	0.90	0.57	0.39	1.45	1.19	0.98	0.34	1.66
09	Buckwheat	4-00-994	88	10.8	1.02	–	–	0.26	0.37	0.56	0.61	0.20	0.20	0.44	–	0.46	0.19	0.54
10	Buttermilk, dried	5-01-160	92	31.6	1.08	0.34	1.39	0.83	2.31	3.10	2.23	0.72	0.40	1.45	0.99	1.47	0.47	2.50
11	Casein, dried	5-01-162	93	87.2	3.61	1.79	5.81	2.78	4.82	9.00	7.99	2.65	0.21	4.96	5.37	4.29	1.05	6.46
12	Casein, dried, coprecipitated	5-20-837	92	85.0	3.42	1.81	5.52	2.52	4.77	8.62	7.31	2.80	0.15	4.81	5.17	4.00	0.98	5.82
13	Corn, yellow	4-02-935	89	8.8	0.50	0.37	0.40	0.20	0.37	1.10	0.24	0.20	0.15	0.47	0.45	0.39	0.09	0.52
14	Corn, ground ear	4-02-849	85	7.8	0.38	0.27	–	0.18	0.35	0.98	0.18	0.14	0.14	0.44	–	0.35	0.07	0.35
	Corn																	
15	Gluten feed	5-02-903	90	22.0	1.01	0.99	0.80	0.71	0.65	1.89	0.63	0.46	0.51	0.77	0.58	0.89	0.10	1.05
16	Gluten meal 41%	5-02-900	91	41.0	1.38	1.50	1.50	0.98	2.18	7.19	0.78	1.03	0.65	2.67	1.00	1.40	0.21	2.23
17	Gluten meal 60%	5-09-318	90	62.0	1.93	1.64	3.07	1.22	2.29	10.11	1.00	1.91	1.11	3.77	2.94	1.97	0.26	2.74
18	Cottonseed meal, expeller	5-01-617	93	40.9	4.26	2.28	–	1.08	1.57	2.47	1.51	0.55	0.59	2.17	0.69	1.38	0.55	1.97
19	Cottonseed meal, solvent	5-07-872	90	41.4	4.59	1.70	–	1.10	1.33	2.41	1.71	0.52	0.64	2.22	1.02	1.32	0.47	1.89
20	Distiller's dried grains w/solubles (corn)	5-02-843	93	27.2	0.98	0.57	1.61	0.66	1.00	2.20	0.75	0.60	0.40	1.20	0.74	0.92	0.19	1.30
21	Distiller's dried solubles (corn)	5-02-844	92	28.5	1.05	1.10	1.30	0.70	1.25	2.11	0.90	0.50	0.40	1.30	0.95	1.00	0.30	1.39
22	Feather meal, hydrolyzed	5-03-795	92	86.4	5.42	6.31	–	0.34	3.26	6.72	1.67	0.42	4.00	3.28	6.31	3.43	0.50	5.57
23	Fish meal, anchovy	5-01-985	92	64.2	3.66	3.59	2.32	1.53	3.01	4.83	4.90	1.93	0.59	2.70	2.18	2.68	0.74	3.38
24	Fish meal, herring	5-02-000	93	72.3	4.84	4.61	2.73	1.70	3.22	5.34	5.70	2.10	0.72	2.79	2.27	3.00	0.81	4.38
25	Fish meal, menhaden	5-02-009	92	60.5	3.79	4.19	2.26	1.46	2.85	4.50	4.83	1.78	0.56	2.48	1.98	2.50	0.68	3.23
26	Fish meal, sardine	5-02-015	92	64.7	3.27	4.52	–	1.78	3.38	5.29	5.90	1.98	0.96	2.29	2.01	2.69	0.68	4.05
27	Fish solubles, condensed	5-01-969	51	31.5	1.61	3.41	0.83	1.56	1.06	1.86	1.73	0.50	0.30	0.93	0.40	0.86	0.31	1.16
28	Fish solubles, dried	5-01-971	92	63.6	2.78	5.89	2.02	2.18	1.95	3.16	3.28	1.00	0.66	1.48	0.78	1.35	0.61	2.22
29	Gelatin	5-14-503	91	88.0	7.4	20.0	2.80	0.85	1.40	3.10	3.70	0.68	0.09	1.70	0.26	1.30	0.09	1.80
30	Hominy feed	4-02-887	90	10.0	0.47	0.40	–	0.20	0.40	0.84	0.40	0.13	0.13	0.35	0.49	0.40	0.10	0.49
31	Liver meal	5-00-389	92	65.6	4.14	5.57	2.49	1.47	3.09	5.28	4.80	1.22	0.89	2.89	1.69	2.48	0.59	4.13

Line No.	Feedstuff	International Feed No.	Dry Matter (%)	Protein (%)	Arginine (%)	Glycine (%)	Serine (%)	Histidine (%)	Iso-leucine (%)	Leucine (%)	Lysine (%)	Methionine (%)	Cystine (%)	Phenylalanine (%)	Tyrosine (%)	Threonine (%)	Tryptophan (%)	Valine (%)
32	Meat and bone meal	5-00-388	93	50.4	3.82	6.79	1.85	0.90	1.40	2.8	2.60	0.85	0.26	1.50	0.76	1.50	0.28	2.00
33	Meat meal	5-00-385	92	54.4	3.73	6.30	1.60	1.30	1.60	3.32	3.00	0.75	0.66	1.70	0.84	1.74	0.36	2.30
34	Oats	4-03-309	89	11.4	0.79	0.50	0.40	0.24	0.52	0.89	0.50	0.18	0.22	0.59	0.53	0.43	0.16	0.68
35	Oats, West coast	4-07-999	91	9.0	0.60	0.40	0.30	0.10	0.40	0.30	0.40	0.13	0.17	0.44	0.20	0.20	0.12	0.51
36	Oat hulls	1-03-281	92	4.6	0.14	0.14	0.14	0.07	0.14	0.26	0.14	0.07	0.08	0.13	0.14	0.13	0.07	0.20
37	Pea, seed	5-33-600	90	23.8	1.40	1.10	–	0.72	1.10	1.80	1.60	0.31	0.17	1.30	–	0.94	0.24	1.30
38	Peanut meal, expeller	5-03-649	90	39.8	5.40	2.20	–	1.10	1.80	3.40	1.80	0.45	0.70	2.60	2.00	1.40	0.50	2.40
39	Peanut meal, solvent	E-03-650	93	50.7	5.50	2.70	2.22	1.19	2.10	2.99	1.76	0.44	0.76	2.75	2.00	1.45	0.65	1.82
40	Poultry by-product meal	5-03-798	93	58.0	4.00	5.90	3.68	1.50	2.00	3.70	2.70	1.00	0.69	2.10	0.54	2.00	0.53	2.60
41	Rapeseed meal, expeller	5-03-870	94	35.0	1.93	1.81	1.48	0.87	1.33	2.31	1.75	0.88	0.31	1.41	0.82	1.53	0.45	1.79
42	Rice bran	4-03-928	91	12.9	0.89	0.80	0.32	0.33	0.52	0.90	0.59	0.20	0.10	0.58	0.68	0.48	0.15	0.75
43	Rice, broken	4-03-932	89	8.7	0.62	0.63	1.36	0.17	0.35	0.52	0.24	0.15	0.08	0.36	–	0.29	0.13	0.50
44	Rice, polishing	4-03-943	90	12.2	0.78	0.71	1.36	0.24	0.41	0.80	0.57	0.22	0.10	0.46	0.63	0.40	0.13	0.76
45	Safflower meal, solvent	5-04-110	91	42.5	2.85	1.12	–	0.44	0.57	1.22	1.30	0.37	0.66	1.16	–	0.56	0.28	1.09
46	Sesame meal, expeller	5-04-220	93	43.8	4.93	4.22	2.96	1.09	2.12	3.33	1.30	1.20	0.59	2.22	2.00	1.65	0.80	2.41
47	Skim milk, dried	5-01-175	93	33.5	1.12	0.27	1.59	0.84	2.15	3.23	2.40	0.93	0.44	1.58	1.13	1.60	0.44	2.30
48	Sorghum, grain (milo)	4-04-444	89	8.9	0.38	0.31	0.53	0.27	0.63	1.42	0.22	0.12	0.15	0.44	0.35	0.27	0.10	0.53
49	Soybeans, heat processed	5-04-597	90	37.0	2.80	2.00	–	0.89	2.00	2.80	2.40	0.51	0.64	1.80	1.20	1.50	0.55	1.80
50	Soybean meal, dehulled	5-04-612	90	48.5	3.68	2.29	2.89	1.32	2.57	3.82	3.18	0.72	0.73	2.11	2.01	1.91	0.67	2.72
51	Soybean meal, expeller	5-04-600	90	42.6	3.00	2.38	2.02	1.10	2.81	3.60	2.78	0.67	0.62	2.12	1.40	1.71	0.61	2.21
52	Soybean meal, solvent	5-04-604	89	44.0	3.28	2.29	2.45	1.16	2.39	3.52	2.93	0.65	0.69	2.27	1.28	1.81	0.62	2.34
53	Soybean mill feed	5-04-594	89	13.3	0.94	0.40	–	0.18	0.40	0.57	0.48	0.10	0.21	0.37	0.23	0.30	0.10	0.37
54	Soybean protein, isolated[b]	5-08-038	93	84.1	6.7	3.3	5.3	2.1	4.6	6.6	5.5	0.81	0.49	4.3	3.1	3.3	0.81	4.4
55	Sunflower meal, solvent, dehulled	5-04-739	93	45.4	3.50	2.69	1.75	1.39	2.78	3.88	1.70	0.72	0.71	2.93	1.19	2.13	0.71	3.24
56	Wheat bran	4-05-190	90	15.7	0.98	0.90	0.90	0.34	0.59	0.91	0.59	0.17	0.25	0.49	0.40	0.42	0.30	0.73
57	Wheat, hard	4-05-268	87	14.1	0.58	0.72	0.63	0.22	0.58	0.94	0.40	0.19	0.26	0.71	0.43	0.37	0.18	0.63
58	Wheat middlings	4-05-205	88	16.0	1.15	0.63	0.75	0.37	0.68	1.07	0.69	0.21	0.32	0.84	0.45	0.49	0.20	0.71
59	Wheat, soft	4-05-337	89	10.2	0.40	0.49	0.55	0.20	0.42	0.69	0.31	0.15	0.22	0.46	0.39	0.32	0.12	0.44
60	Whey, dried	4-01-182	93	12.0	0.34	0.30	0.32	0.18	0.82	1.19	0.97	0.19	0.30	0.33	0.26	0.89	0.19	0.68
61	Whey, product, dried	4-01-186	91	16.5	0.67	1.04	0.76	0.10	0.90	1.15	1.47	0.57	0.57	0.50	0.20	0.50	0.18	0.30
62	Yeast, brewer's, dried	7-05-527	93	44.4	2.19	2.09	–	1.07	2.14	3.19	3.23	0.70	0.50	1.81	1.49	2.06	0.49	2.32
63	Yeast, torula, dried	7-05-534	93	47.2	2.60	2.60	–	1.40	2.90	3.50	3.80	0.80	0.60	3.00	2.10	2.60	0.50	2.90

[a] As-fed basis.
[b] Soybean protein concentrate (AAFCO).

TABLE 20   Energy, Fat,[a] and Linoleic Acid Composition of Feed Ingredients[b]

Ingredient	International Feed No.	Dry Matter (%)	Ether Extract (%)	Energy (kcal/kg) ME_n	Pro	Linoleic Acid (%)
Corn oil	4-07-882	100	100	8,820		55.0
Corn starch	4-02-889	90	0.0	3,650	2,916	0.0
Corn, yellow	4-02-935	89	4.8	3,430		2.0
Cottonseed oil	4-20-836	100	100	8,800		53.0
Fish meal, manhaden	5-02-009	91	9.0	2,720		0.1
Glucose monohydrate	4-02-125	91	0.0	3,300	2,386	0.0
Meat meal	5-00-385	92	7.0	2,000		0.3
Molasses, beet	4-00-668	77	0.0	1,930		0.0
Molasses, cane, dried	4-04-695	93	0.0	2,340		0.0
Poultry oil	4-00-409	100	100	8,170		22.3
Rapeseed oil, high erucic	4-20-835	100	100	8,700		17.0
Rapeseed oil, low erucic	4-20-834	100	100	8,800		19.7
Safflower oil	4-14-505	100	100	8,800		72.7
Soybean oil	4-07-983	100	100	8,820		51.9
Sucrose	4-04-701	100	0.0	3,680	2,763	0.0
Sunflower oil	4-20-833	100	100	8,815		51.0
Tallow	4-08-127	100	100	7,050		4.3
Wheat	4-05-282	87	2.0	2,610		1.1
White grease	4-04-790	100	100	8,600		18.3

[a]Several blends of animal-vegetable fats are available. Manufacturers provide specifications and fatty-acid composition of these products.
[b]As-fed basis.

TABLE 21   Calcium, Phosphorus, Sodium, Fluoride, and Selenium Content of Common Mineral Sources

Ingredient	International Feed No.	Calcium (%)	Phosphorus (%)	Sodium (%)	Fluoride (%)	Selenium (ppm)
Bone meal	6-00-400	29	12.6	0.37	0.06	
Calcium carbonate	6-01-069	38	0	0.02	0	0
Fish meal, manhaden	5-02-009	5.1	2.9	0.4[a]	0.01	1.7
Limestone, ground[b]	6-02-632	38	0	0.06	0.01	0.2
Meat and bone meal	5-00-385	8.3	4.1	1.4	0.05	0.3
Oyster shell	6-03-481	38	0	0.2	0.29	0
Phosphate, curacao	6-05-586	36	14	0.3[a]	0.54	2.0
Phosphate, defluorinated	6-01-780	32	18	5.7[a]	0.16	1.4
Phosphate, dicalcium	6-01-080	21	18.5	0.6[a]	0.14	0.2
Phosphate, mono- + dicalcium	6-01-061	16	21	0.6[a]	0.20	
Phosphate, soft rock	6-03-947	17	9	0.1	1.2	0.3
Sodium chloride	6-14-013	0	0	39.3	0	0

[a]Some contain different sodium levels. Check with manufacturer.
[b]High calcium.

BIBLIOGRAPHY

AMINO ACIDS

Adams, R. L., F. N. Andrews, J. C. Rogler, and C. W. Carrick. 1962. The sulfur amino acid requirement of the chick from four to eight weeks of age as affected by temperature. Poult. Sci. 41:1801–1806.

Adkins, J. S., E. C. Miller, H. R. Bird, C. A. Elvehjem, and M. L. Sunde. 1958. An estimate of the threonine requirement of the laying hen. Poult. Sci. 37:1362–1367.

Adkins, J. S., A. E. Harper, and M. L. Sunde. 1962. The l-arginine requirement of the laying pullet. Poult. Sci. 41:657–663.

Almquist, H. J. 1952. Amino acid requirements of chickens and turkeys—a review. Poult. Sci. 31:966–981.

Anderson, J. O., and C. I. Draper. 1956. Protein supplements for laying rations high in wheat. Poult. Sci. 35:562–566.

Balloun, S. L. 1962. Lysine, arginine, and methionine balance of diets for turkeys to 24 weeks of age. Poult. Sci. 41:417–424.

Bauriedel, W. R. 1963. The effect of feeding d-methionine on the d-amino acid oxidase of chick tissues. Poult. Sci. 42:214–217.

Boomgaardt, J., and D. H. Baker. 1973. The lysine requirement of growing chicks fed sesame meal-gelatin diets at three protein levels. Poult. Sci. 52:586–591.

Boomgaardt, J., and D. H. Baker. 1973. Effect of age on the lysine and sulfur amino acid requirement of growing chicks. Poult. Sci. 52:592–597.

Bray, D. J. 1969. Studies with corn-soya laying diets. Poult. Sci. 48:674–684.

Carew, L. B., and F. W. Hill. 1961. Effect of methionine deficiency on the utilization of energy by the chick. J. Nutr. 74:185–190.

Carlson, C. W., and E. Guenther. 1969. Response of laying hens fed typical corn-soy diets to supplements of methionine and lysine. Poult. Sci. 48:137–143.

Carter, R. D., E. C. Naber, S. P. Touchburn, J. W. Wyne, V. D. Chamberlin, and M. G. McCartney. 1962. Amino acid supplementation of low-protein turkey growing rations. Poult. Sci. 41:305–311.

Chi, M. S., and G. M. Speers. 1976. Effects of dietary protein and lysine levels on plasma amino acids, nitrogen retention and egg production in laying hens. J. Nutr. 106:1192–1201.

Choudhury, H., and C. W. Carlson. 1972. Isoleucine, threonine and valine supplementation of low protein diets for layers. Poult. Sci. 51:1794. (Abstr.)

Combs, G. F. 1961. Maryland broiler nutrition studies. Proc. Md. Nutr. Conf., pp. 51–64.

Combs, G. F. 1962. Maryland nutrition studies with broilers and laying hens. Proc. Md. Nutr. Conf., pp. 65–87.

Combs, G. F. 1970. Feed ingredient composition and amino acid standards for broilers. Proc. Md. Nutr. Conf., pp. 81–89.

Dean, W. F., and H. M. Scott. 1965. The development of an amino acid reference diet for the early growth of chicks. Poult. Sci. 44:803–808.

Edwards, H. M., Jr., L. C. Norris, and G. F. Heuser. 1956. Studies on the lysine requirement of chicks. Poult. Sci. 35:385–390.

Fisher, C., and T. R. Morris. 1970. The determination of the methionine requirement of laying pullets by a diet dilution technique. Br. Poult. Sci. 11:67–82.

Fisher, H., D. Johnson, Jr., and G. A. Leveille. 1957. The phenylalanine and tyrosine requirement of the growing chick with special reference to the utilization of the d-isomer of phenylalanine. J. Nutr. 62:349–355.

Fisher, H., P. Griminger, and G. A. Leveille. 1959. Protein depletion and amino acid requirement in the growing chicken. J. Nutr. 69:117–120.

Fisher, H., P. Griminger, and H. Lutz. 1960a. The amino acid requirement of laying hens. Poult. Sci. 39:173–175.

Fisher, H., P. Griminger, and R. Shapiro. 1960b. Quantitative aspects of lysine deficiency and amino acid imbalance. J. Nutr. 71:213–220.

Fitzsimmons, R. C., and P. E. Waibel. 1962. Determination of the limiting amino acids in corn-soybean oil meal diets for young turkeys. Poult. Sci. 41:260–268.

Gazo, M., V. Gergelyiova, and A. Grom. 1970. Lysine requirement of fattening ducklings. Sitzungsber. Dtsch. Akad. Landwirtschafts-Wiss. 19(3):59–63.

Graber, C., and D. H. Baker. 1973. The essential nature of glycine and proline for growing chicks. Poult. Sci. 52:892–896.

Greene, D. E., H. M. Scott, and B. C. Johnson. 1960. A need for glycine in crystalline amino acid diets. Poult. Sci. 39:512–514.

Greene, D. E., H. M. Scott, and B. C. Johnson. 1962. The role of proline and certain non-essential amino acids in chick nutrition. Poult. Sci. 41:116–120.

Griminger, P., and H. Fisher. 1962. Genetic differences in growth potential on amino acid deficient diets. Proc. Soc. Exp. Biol. Med. 111:754–756.

Griminger, P., and H. M. Scott. 1959. Growth rate and lysine requirement of the chick. J. Nutr. 68:429–442.

49

Harms, R. H., and B. L. Damron. 1969. Protein and sulfur amino acid requirement of the laying hen as influenced by dietary formulation. Poult. Sci. 48:144–149.

Harms, R. H., C. R. Douglas, and P. W. Waldroup. 1962. Methionine supplementation of laying hen diets. Poult. Sci. 41:805–812.

Hewitt, D., and D. Lewis. 1972. The amino acid requirements of the growing chicks. 1. Determination of amino acid requirements. Br. Poult. Sci. 13:449–463.

Heywang, B. W., M. G. Vavich, and B. L. Reid. 1963. Supplemental methionine in a sixteen percent protein diet for laying chickens. Poult. Sci. 42:245–249.

Hurwitz, S., and S. Bornstein. 1973. The protein and amino acid requirements of laying hens: suggested models for calculation. Poult. Sci. 52:1124–1134.

Jensen, L. S., C. H. Change, and L. Falen. 1974a. Response to lysine supplementation by laying hens fed practical diets. Poult. Sci. 53:1387–1391.

Jensen, L. S., L. Falen, and G. W. Schumaier. 1974b. Requirement of White Leghorn laying and breeding hens for methionine as influenced by stage of production cycle and inorganic sulfate. Poult. Sci. 53:535–544.

Johnson, D., Jr., and H. Fisher. 1958. The amino acid requirement of laying hens. Br. J. Nutr. 12:276–285.

Kim, S. M., and J. McGinnis. 1972. Methionine requirement of white leghorn pullets. Poult. Sci. 51:1735–1740.

Klain, G. J., H. M. Scott, and B. C. Johnson. 1960. The amino acid requirement of the growing chick fed a crystalline amino acid diet. Poult. Sci. 39:39–44.

Kummero, V. E., J. E. Jones, and C. B. Loadholt. 1971. Lysine and total sulfur amino acid requirements of turkey poults, one day to three weeks. Poult. Sci. 50:752–758.

Leong, K. C., M. L. Sunde, H. R. Bird, and C. A. Elvehjem. 1959. Interrelationships among dietary energy, protein and amino acids for chickens. Poult. Sci. 38:1267–1285.

March, B. E., and J. Biely. 1972. The effects of protein level and amino acid balance in wheat-based laying rations. Poult. Sci. 51:547–557.

Muller, R. D., and S. L. Balloun. 1972. Amino acid supplementation of corn-soy laying hen diets. Poult. Sci. 51:1843. (Abstr.)

Muller, R. D., and S. L. Balloun. 1973. Further studies with methionine additions and leucine imbalance in corn-soybean meal laying hen diets. Poult. Sci. 52:2068. (Abstr.)

Muller, R. D., and S. L. Balloun. 1974. Response to methionine supplementation of leghorn hens fed low-protein corn-soybean meal diets. Poult. Sci. 53:1463–1475.

Nelson, T. S., R. M. Young, R. B. Bradfield, J. B. Anderson, L. C. Norris, F. W. Hill, and M. L. Scott. 1960. Studies on the sulfur amino acid requirement of the chick. Poult. Sci. 39:308–314.

Nesheim, M. C., and F. B. Hutt. 1962. Genetic differences among White Leghorn chicks in requirements of arginine. Science 137:691–692.

Owings, W. J., and S. L. Balloun. 1959. Relation of arginine and lysine to feather tyrosinase activity. Poult. Sci. 38:1285–1289.

Patterson, E. L., R. A. Milstrey, and T. H. Jukes. 1961. Arginine in the growth of chicks. Poult. Sci. 40:459–467.

Petersen, C. F., E. A. Sauter, and E. E. Steele. 1971. Protein and methionine requirements for early egg production. Poult. Sci. 50:1617. (Abstr.)

Reid, B. L., and C. W. Weber. 1973. Dietary protein and sulfur amino acid levels for laying hens during heat stress. Poult. Sci. 52:1335–1343.

Roberson, R. H., and D. W. Francis. 1966. The lysine requirement of white Chinese goslings. Poult. Sci. 45:324–329.

Rosenberg, H. R., J. T. Baldini, and C. I. Tollefson. 1957. Histidine requirement of the growing chick. Poult. Sci. 36:1381–1382.

Sasse, C. F., and D. H. Baker. 1974. Factors affecting sulfate-sulfur utilization by the young chick. Poult. Sci. 53:652–662.

Savage, J. E., and B. L. O'Dell. 1960. Arginine requirement of the chick and the arginine sparing value of related compounds. J. Nutr. 70:129–134.

Scott, M. L., E. R. Holm, and R. E. Reynolds. 1963. Studies on the protein and methionine requirements of young bobwhite quail and young ringnecked pheasants. Poult. Sci. 42:676–680.

Svacha, A. J., C. W. Weber, and B. L. Reid. 1969. Lysine, methionine and glycine requirements of growing Coturnix quail. Poult. Sci. 48:1881. (Abstr.)

Svacha, A., C. W. Weber, and B. L. Reid. 1970. Lysine, methionine and glycine requirements of Japanese quail to five weeks of age. Poult. Sci. 49:54–59.

Tuttle, W. L., and S. L. Balloun. 1974. Lysine requirements of starting and growing turkeys. Poult. Sci. 53:1698–1704.

Twining, P. V., Jr., O. P. Thomas, E. H. Bossard, and J. L. Nicholson. 1973. The available lysine requirement of 7–9 week old male broiler chicks. Poult. Sci. 52:2280–2286.

Waibel, P. E. 1959. Methionine and lysine in rations for turkey poults under various dietary conditions. Poult. Sci. 38:712–721.

Waibel, P. E. 1968. Amino acids and protein for growing turkeys. Minn. Nutr. Conf. Proc., p. 149.

Warnick, R. E., and J. O. Anderson. 1973. Essential amino acid levels for starting turkey poults. Poult. Sci. 52:445–452.

Waterhouse, H. N., and H. M. Scott. 1961. Glycine need of the chick fed casein diets and the glycine, arginine, methionine and creatine interrelationships. J. Nutr. 73:266–272.

ANTIBIOTICS AND ARSENIC COMPOUNDS

Al-Timimi, A. A., and T. W. Sullivan. 1972. Safety and toxicity of dietary organic arsenicals relative to performance of young turkeys. 1. Arsanilic acid and sodium arsanilate. Poult. Sci. 51:111–116.

Bare, L. N., R. F. Wiseman, and O. J. Abbott. 1964. Effect of dietary antibiotics on coliform bacteria and lactobacilli in the intestinal tract of uric acid-fed chicks. J. Bacteriol. 87:329–331.

Coates, M. E., C. D. Dickinson, G. F. Harrison, S. K. Kon, J. W. G. Porter, S. H. Cummins, and W. F. J. Cuthbertson. 1952. A mode of action of antibiotics in chick nutrition. J. Sci. Food Agric. 3:43–48.

Elam, J. F., R. L. Jacobs, and J. R. Couch. 1953a. The effect of prolonged feeding of antibiotics upon the performance of laying hens. Poult. Sci. 32:792–795.

Elam, J. F., R. L. Jacobs, W. L. Tidwell, L. L. Gee, and J. R. Couch. 1953b. Possible mechanism involved in the growth promoting responses obtained from antibiotics. J. Nutr. 49:307–318.

Eyssen, H., and P. DeSomer. 1963. The mode of action of antibiotics in stimulating growth of chicks. J. Exp. Med. 117:127–138.

Frost, D. B. 1953. Considerations on the safety of arsanilic acid for use in poultry feeds. Poult. Sci. 32:217–227.

Heth, D. A., and H. R. Bird. 1962. Growth responses of chicks to antibiotics from 1950 to 1961. Poult. Sci. 41:755–760.

Heywang, B. W. 1959. The effect of arsanilic acid and low levels of antibiotics on laying chickens during hot weather. Poult. Sci. 38:854–858.

Huhtanen, C. M., and J. M. Pensack. 1965. The role of *Streptococcus faecalis* in the antibiotic growth effect in chickens. Poult. Sci. 44:830–834.

March, B. E., A. Akinwande, and R. Soong. 1972. The effect of feeding antibiotics for different periods on growth rate, feed conversion and metabolizability of dietary energy in growing chickens. Poult. Sci. 51:1409–1414.

Nivas, S. C., M. L. Sunde, and H. R. Bird. 1967. Erythromycin thiocyanate and the performance of laying hens. Poult. Sci. 46:1103–1108.

Report of the Joint Committee on the Use of Antibiotics in Animal Husbandry and Veterinary Medicine (Swann Report). 1968. H. M. Stationary Office, London, England.

Richmond, M. H. 1972. Some environmental consequences of the use of antibiotics. J. Appl. Bacteriol. 35:155–176.

Stokstad, E. L. R., and T. H. Jukes. 1950. Further observations on the "animal protein factor." Proc. Soc. Exp. Biol. Med. 73:523–528.

Sullivan, T. W., and A. A. Al-Timimi. 1972a. Safety and toxicity of dietary organic arsenicals relative to the performance of young turkeys. 2. Carbarsone. Poult. Sci. 51:1498–1501.

Sullivan, T. W., and A. A. Al-Timimi. 1972b. Safety and toxicity of dietary organic arsenicals relative to the performance of young turkeys. 3. Nitarsone. Poult. Sci. 51:1582–1586.

Specifications for the identity and purity of food additives and their toxicological evaluation: some antibiotics. 1968. 12th Report of the Joint FAO/WHO Expert Committee in Food Additives. FAO, Rome.

BIOTIN

Anderson, J. O., and R. E. Warnick. 1970. Studies of the need for supplemental biotin in chick rations. Poult. Sci. 49:569–578.

Arends, L. G., E. W. Kienholz, J. V. Shutze, and D. D. Taylor. 1971. Effect of supplemental biotin on reproductive performance of turkey breeder hens and its effect on the subsequent progeny's performance. Poult. Sci. 50:206–214.

Brewer, L. E., and H. M. Edwards, Jr. 1972. Studies on the biotin requirement of broiler breeders. Poult. Sci. 51:619–624.

Couch, J. R., W. W. Cravens, C. A. Elvehjem, and J. G. Halpin. 1948. Relation of biotin to congenital deformities in the chick. Anat. Rec. 100:29–48.

Couch, J. R., W. W. Cravens, C. A. Elvehjem, and J. G. Halpin. 1949. Studies on the function of biotin in the domestic fowl. Arch. Biochem. 21:77–86.

Cravens, W. W., E. E. Sebesta, J. G. Halpin, and E. B. Hart. 1942. Effect of biotin on reproduction in the domestic fowl. Proc. Soc. Exp. Biol. Med. 50:101–104.

Dobson, D. C. 1970. Biotin requirement of turkey poults. Poult. Sci. 49:546–553.

Hegsted, D. M., R. C. Mills, G. M. Briggs, Jr., C. A. Elvehjem, and E. B. Hart. 1942. Biotin in chick nutrition. J. Nutr. 23:175–179.

Jensen, L. S., and R. Martinson. 1969. Requirement of turkey poults for biotin and effect of deficiency on incidence of leg weakness in developing turkeys. Poult. Sci. 48:222–230.

Marusich, W. L., E. F. Ogrinz, M. Brand, and M. Mitrovic. 1970. Induction, prevention and therapy of biotin deficiency in turkey poults on semipurified and commercial-type rations. Poult. Sci. 49:412–421.

Patrick, H., R. V. Boucher, R. A. Dutcher, and H. C. Knandel. 1942. The nutritional significance of biotin in chick and poult nutrition. Poult. Sci. 21:476. (Abstr.)

Payne, C. G., P. Gilchrist, J. A. Pearson, and L. A. Hemsley. 1974. Involvement of biotin in the fatty liver and kidney syndrome of broilers. Br. Poult. Sci. 15:489–498.

Waibel, P. E., L. M. Krista, R. L. Arnold, L. G. Blaylock, and L. H. Neagle. 1969. Effect of supplementary biotin on performance of turkeys fed corn-soybean meal type diets. Poult. Sci. 48:1979–1985.

CALCIUM (AND PHOSPHORUS)

Aitken, J. R., G. S. Lindblad, and W. G. Hunsaker. 1958. The calcium and phosphorus requirements of goslings. Poult. Sci. 37:1180. (Abstr.)

Berg, L. R., G. E. Bearse, and L. H. Merrill. 1962. Effect of calcium level of the developing and laying ration on hatchability of eggs and on viability and growth rate of progeny of young pullets. Poult. Sci. 41:1328–1335.

Berg, L. R., G. E. Bearse, and L. H. Merrill. 1964. The calcium and phosphorus requirement of White Leghorn pullets from 8–21 weeks. Poult. Sci. 43:885–896.

Bethke, R. M., D. C. Kennard, C. H. Kik, and G. Zinzalian. 1929. The calcium-phosphorus relationship in the nutrition of the growing chick. Poult. Sci. 8:257–265.

Consuegra, P. F., and D. L. Anderson. 1967. Studies on the dietary calcium and phosphorus requirements of immature Coturnix quail. Poult. Sci. 46:1247. (Abstr.)

Day, E. J., and B. C. Dilworth. 1962. Dietary phosphorus levels and calcium: phosphorus ratios needed by growing turkeys. Poult. Sci. 41:1324–1328.

Dean, W. F., M. L. Scott, R. J. Young, and W. J. Ash. 1967. Calcium requirement of ducklings. Poult. Sci. 46:1496–1499.

DeWitt, J. B., R. B. Nestler, and J. V. Derby, Jr. 1949. Calcium and phosphorus requirements of breeding bobwhite quail. J. Nutr. 39:567–577.

Evans, R. J., and J. S. Carver. 1942. The calcium and phosphorus requirements of Single Comb White Leghorn pullets. Poult. Sci. 21:469. (Abstr.)

Ferguson, T. M., C. E. Sewell, and R. L. Atkinson. 1974. Phosphorous levels in the turkey breeder diet. Poult. Sci. 53:1627–1629.

Fritz, J. C., T. Roberts, J. W. Boehne, and E. L. Hove. 1969. Factors affecting the chick's requirement for phosphorus. Poult. Sci. 48:307–320.

Nelson, R. E., L. S. Jensen, and J. McGinnis. 1961. Requirement of developing turkeys for calcium and phosphorus. Poult. Sci. 40:407–411.

Norris, L. C., G. F. Heuser, A. T. Ringrose, and H. S. Wilgus. 1934. Studies of the calcium requirement of laying hens. Poult. Sci. 13:308–309. (Abstr.)

Petersen, C. F., D. H. Conrad, D. H. Lumijarvi, E. A. Sauter, and C. E. Lampman. 1960. Studies on the calcium requirements of high producing White Leghorn hens. Idaho Univ. Agric. Exp. Stn. Bull. 44.

Potter, L. M., A. T. Leighton, and A. B. Chu. 1974. Calcium, phosphorus, and Nopgro as variables in diets of breeder turkeys. Poult. Sci. 53:15–22.

Scott, M. L., E. R. Holm, and R. E. Reynolds. 1958. The calcium, phosphorus and vitamin D requirements of young pheasants. Poult. Sci. 37:1419–1425.

Sullivan, T. W. 1960. An estimate of the phosphorus requirement of Broad Breasted Bronze turkeys, 8–20 weeks of age. Poult. Sci. 39:1321–1327.

Waibel, P. E., E. L. Johnson, and A. M. Pilkey. 1961. Successful turkey growth with reduced calcium and phosphorus levels. Poult. Sci. 40:256–258.

Waldroup, P. W., C. B. Ammerman, and R. H. Harms. 1963. The relationship of phosphorus, calcium and vitamin D₃ in the diet of broiler-type chicks. Poult. Sci. 42:982–989.

Waldroup, P. W., J. F. Maxey, and L. W. Luther. 1974. Studies on the calcium and phosphorus requirements of caged turkey breeder hens. Poult. Sci. 53:886–888.

Wilcox, R. A., C. W. Carlson, and W. Kohlmeyer. 1961. Effects of phosphorus supplementation on growing turkeys as measured by body weight and toe ash. Poult. Sci. 40:1533–1536.

Wilgus, H. S. 1931. The quantitative requirement of the growing chick for calcium and phosphorus. Poult. Sci. 10:107–117.

CHOLINE

Balloun, S. L. 1956. Choline and tallow in breeder-hen diets. Poult. Sci. 35:737–738.

Deeb, S. S., and P. A. Thornton. 1959. The choline requirement of the chick. Poult. Sci. 38:1198. (Abstr.)

Evans, R. J. 1943. The choline requirements of turkey poults. Poult. Sci. 22:266–267.

Gillis, M. B., and L. C. Norris. 1949. Vitamin B₁₂ and the requirement of the chick for methylating compounds. Poult. Sci. 28:749–750.

Johnson, E. L. 1954. Vitamin B₁₂ requirements of hens as affected by choline and penicillin. Poult. Sci. 33:100–107.

Latshaw, J. D., and L. S. Jensen. 1971. Choline level and its effect on egg weight in the Japanese quail. Poult. Sci. 50:790–794.

Latshaw, J. D., and L. S. Jensen. 1972. Choline deficiency and synthesis of choline from precursors in mature Japanese quail. J. Nutr. 102:749–755.

Lucas, H. L., L. C. Norris, and G. F. Heuser. 1946. Observations on the choline requirements of hens. Poult. Sci. 25:373–375.

Nesheim, M. C., M. J. Norvell, E. Ceballos, and R. M. Leach, Jr. 1971. The effect of choline supplementation of diets for growing pullets and laying hens. Poult. Sci. 50:820–831.

Record, P. R., and R. M. Bethke. 1942. Further observations on choline and yeast in chick nutrition. Poult. Sci. 21:271–276.

Ringrose, R. C., and H. A. Davis. 1946. Choline in the nutrition of laying hens. Poult. Sci. 25:646–647.

Schaefer, A. E., W. D. Salmon, and D. R. Strength. 1949. Interrelationship of vitamin B₁₂ and choline. Proc. Soc. Exp. Biol. Med. 71:202–204.

Scott, M. L., E. R. Holm, and R. E. Reynolds. 1959. Studies on the niacin, riboflavin, choline, manganese and zinc requirements of young ringnecked pheasants for growth, feathering and prevention of leg disorders. Poult. Sci. 38:1344–1350.

Serafin, J. A. 1974. Studies on the riboflavin, niacin, pantothenic acid and choline requirements of young Bobwhite quail. Poult. Sci. 53:1522–1532.

Singsen, E. P., L. D. Matterson, A. Kozeff, and L. Decker. 1950. The choline requirements of turkey breeders. Poult. Sci. 29:780. (Abstr.)

Vogt, Von H. 1970. Choline requirement of quail. Arch. Gefluegelkd. 34:41–44.

Welch, B. E., and J. R. Couch. 1955. Homocystine, vitamin B₁₂, choline and methionine in the nutrition of the laying fowl. Poult. Sci. 34:214–222.

West, J. W., C. W. Carrick, S. M. Hauge, and E. T. Mertz. 1951. The relationship of choline and cystine to the methionine requirement of young chickens. Poult. Sci. 30:880–885.

ENERGY

Anderson, D. L. 1955. The energy values of poultry feed. Proc. 1955 Cornell Nutr. Conf., pp. 5–10.

Anderson, D. L., F. W. Hill, and R. Renner. 1958. Studies of metabolizable and production energy of glucose for the growing chick. J. Nutr. 65:561–574.

Carew, L. B., and F. W. Hill. 1964. Effect of corn oil on metabolic efficiency of energy utilization by chicks. J. Nutr. 83:293–299.

DeGroote, G. 1974. A comparison of a new net energy system with the metabolizable energy system in broiler diet formulation, performance and profitability. Br. Poult. Sci. 15:75–95.

Ewan, R. C. 1976. Utilization of energy of feed ingredients by young pigs. Distill. Feed Res. Counc. Proc. 31:16–21.

Fraps, G. S. 1946. Composition and productive energy of poultry feeds and rations. Tex. Agric. Exp. Stn. Bull. 678.

Fuller, H. L. 1975. Limitations in the use of metabolizable energy values. Proc. 1975 Ga. Nutr. School, pp. 2–8.

Hill, F. W., and D. L. Anderson. 1958. Comparison of metabolizable energy and productive energy determinations with growing chicks. J. Nutr. 64:587–603.

Hill, F. W., and R. Renner. 1957. Metabolizable energy values of feedstuffs for poultry and their use in formulation of rations. Proc. 1957 Cornell Nutr. Conf., pp. 22–32.

Jensen, L. S. 1974. Calorie efficiency of fats versus carbohydrates for poultry. International Symposium on Energy Management in Mixed Feeds, Luxembourg.

Matterson, L. D., L. M. Potter, M. W. Stutz, and E. P. Singsen. 1965. The metabolizable energy of feed ingredients for chicken. Agric. Exp. Stn. Univ. Conn. Res. Rep. 7.

Potter, L. M., and L. D. Matterson. 1960. Metabolizable energy of feed ingredients for growing turkeys. Poult. Sci. 39:781–782.

Sibbald, I. R. 1975. The level of feed intake on metabolizable energy values measured with adult roosters. Poult. Sci. 54:1990–1997.

Sibbald, I. R. 1976a. A bioassay for true metabolizable energy in feedstuffs. Poult. Sci. 55:303–308.

Sibbald, I. R. 1976b. The true metabolizable energy value of several feedstuffs measured with roosters, laying hens, turkeys and broiler hens. Poult. Sci. 55:1459–1463.

Sibbald, I. R., and S. J. Slinger. 1962. The metabolizable energy of materials fed to growing chicks. Poult. Sci. 41:1612–1613.

Stutz, M. W., and L. D. Matterson. 1962. Metabolizable energy of animal by-products for the growing chick. Poult. Sci. 41:1617–1619.

Titus, H. W. 1961. The scientific feeding of chickens, 4th ed. Interstate Press, Danville, Ill.

FEED REQUIREMENTS, SYSTEMS, AND RESTRICTIONS

Andrews, L. D., and L. T. Lankford. 1969. Arkansas meat performance egg phase and reproduction test no. 13, Ark. Agric. Exp. Stn. Rep. Ser. 183.

Byerly, T. C. 1941. Feed and other costs of producing market eggs. Md. Univ. Agric. Exp. Stn. Bull. A1 (technical).

Gowe, R. S., A. S. Johnson, R. D. Crawford, J. H. Downs, A. T. Hill, W. F. Mountain, J. R. Pelletier, and J. H. Strain. 1960. Restricted versus full-feeding during the growing period for egg production stock. Br. Poult. Sci. 1:37–56.

Isaacks, R. E., B. C. Reid, R. E. Davies, J. H. Quisenberry, and

J. R. Couch. 1960. Restricted feeding broiler type replacement stock. Poult. Sci. 39:339–346.

Jensen, L. S. 1975. 1975 Turkey feed consumption standards recognize seasonal differences. Turkey World (January, pp. 26–28.

Parsons, R. 1969. This broiler business. Which weight, when? Poult. Meat 20(12):6.

Proudfoot, F. G., and R. S. Gowe. 1974. The influence of an increased photoperiod, a modified natural day length and feed restriction during the rearing period on the performance of five S.C.W.L. genotypes. Poult. Sci. 53:518–528.

Singsen, E. P., L. D. Matterson, J. Tlustohowez, and L. M. Potter. 1958. The effect of controlled feeding, energy intake and type of diet on the performance of heavy type laying hens. Conn. Agric. Exp. Stn. Bull. 346.

Snetsinger, D., and R. Zimmerman. 1974. Limited feeding of egg strain layers. Feedstuffs 48(4):70–93.

Sunde, M. L., and J. L. Skinner. Fact Sheet Poultry Series No. 41. University of Wisconsin Extension Service, Madison, Wis.

Touchburn, S. P., E. C. Naber, and V. D. Chamberlin. 1968. Effect of growth restriction on reproductive performance of turkeys. Poult. Sci. 47:547–556.

Wilson, H. R., J. L. Fry, R. H. Harms, and L. R. Arrington. 1967. Performance of hens molted by various methods. Poult. Sci. 46:1406–1412.

FOLACIN

Campbell, C. F., R. A. Brown, and A. D. Emmett. 1944. Influence of crystalline vitamin Bc on hematopoiesis in the chick. J. Biol. Chem. 152:483–484.

Couch, J. R., and H. L. German. 1950. Pteroylglutamic acid studies with the mature fowl. Poult. Sci. 29:539–544.

Cravens, W. W., and J. G. Halpin. 1949. The effect of pteroylglutamic acid and an unidentified factor on egg production and hatchability. J. Nutr. 37:127–138.

Creek, R. D., and V. Vasaitis. 1963. The effect of excess dietary protein on the need for folic acid by the chick. Poult. Sci. 42:1136–1141.

Hutchings, B. L., J. J. Oleson, and E. L. R. Stokstad. 1946. The *Lactobacillus casei* factors in the nutrition of the chick. J. Biol. Chem. 163:447–453.

Jukes, T. H., E. L. R. Stokstad, and M. Belt. 1947. Deficiencies of certain vitamins as studied with turkey poults on a purified diet. J. Nutr. 33:1–12.

Kratzer, F. H., P. N. Davis, and U. P. Abbott. 1956. The folic acid requirement of turkey breeder hens. Poult. Sci. 35:711–716.

Lillie, R. J., and G. M. Briggs. 1947. Folic acid requirements of New Hampshire chicks receiving synthetic diets. Poult. Sci. 26:295–298.

Luckey, T. D., P. R. Moore, C. A. Elvehjem, and E. B. Hart. 1946. The activity of synthetic folic acid in purified rations for the chick. Science 103:682–684.

March, B. E., and J. Biely. 1955. Fat studies in poultry. 3. Folic acid and fat tolerance in the chick. Poult. Sci. 34:39–44.

March, B. E., and J. Biely. 1956. Folic acid supplementation of high-protein, high-fat diets. Poult. Sci. 35:550–551.

Oleson, J. J., B. L. Hutchings, and N. H. Sloane. 1946. The effect of the synthetic pteroylglutamic acid on the feathering of chickens. J. Biol. Chem. 165:371–375.

Robertson, E. I., L. J. Daniel, F. A. Farmer, L. C. Norris, and G. F. Heuser. 1946. Folic acid requirement of growing chicks. Poult. Sci. 25:411. (Abstr.)

Russell, W. C., M. W. Taylor, and J. V. Derby, Jr. 1947. The folic acid requirement of turkey poults on a purified diet. J. Nutr. 34:621–632.

Sauberlich, H. E., and A. E. Schaefer. 1953. Studies on aminopterin, leucovorin and folacin with the chick. Poult. Sci. 33:107–111.

Saxena, H. C., G. E. Bearse, C. F. McClary, L. G. Blaylock, and L. R. Berg. 1954. Deficiency of folic acid in rations containing natural feedstuffs. Poult. Sci. 33:815–820.

Schweigert, B. S., H. L. German, P. B. Pearson, and R. M. Sherwood. 1947. Effect of the pteroylglutamic acid intake on the performance of turkeys and chickens. J. Nutr. 35:89–102.

Scott, M. L., G. F. Heuser, and L. C. Norris. 1948. Studies in turkey nutrition using a purified diet. Poult. Sci. 27:770–772.

Taylor, L. W. 1947. The effect of folic acid on egg production and hatchability. Poult. Sci. 26:372–376.

Totter, J. R., W. E. Martindale, M. McKee, C. K. Keith, and P. L. Day. 1949. Biochemical studies on livers of chicks receiving graded levels of pteroylglutamic acid. Proc. Soc. Exp. Biol. Med. 70:435–438.

Young, R. J., L. C. Norris, and G. F. Heuser. 1955. The chick's requirement for folic acid in the utilization of choline and its precursors betaine and methylaminoethanol. J. Nutr. 55:353–362.

IODINE

Creek, R. D., H. E. Parker, S. M. Hauge, F. N. Andrews, and C. W. Carrick. 1957. The iodine requirements of young chickens. Poult. Sci. 36:1360–1365.

Rogler, J. C., H. E. Parker, F. N. Andrews, and C. W. Carrick. 1961. The iodine requirements of the breeding hen. Poult. Sci. 40:1546–1562.

Scott, M. L., A. van Tienhoven, E. R. Holm, and R. E. Reynolds. 1960. Studies on the sodium, chlorine and iodine requirements of young pheasants and quail. J. Nutr. 71:282–288.

Wilgus, H. S., G. S. Harshfield, A. R. Patton, L. P. Ferris, and F. X. Gassner. 1941. The iodine requirements of growing chickens. Poult. Sci. 20:477. (Abstr.)

IRON AND COPPER

Al-Ubaidi, Y. Y., and T. W. Sullivan. 1963. Studies on the requirements and interaction of copper and iron in Broad Breasted Bronze turkeys to 4 weeks of age. Poult. Sci. 42:718–725.

Carlton, W. W., and W. Henderson. 1964. Studies on the copper requirements of growing chicks. Avian Dis. 8:227–234.

Davis, P. N., L. C. Norris, and F. H. Kratzer. 1968. Iron utilization and metabolism in the chick. J. Nutr. 94:407–417.

Fritz, J. C., W. Bochne, and T. Roberts. 1969. A study of the chick's requirements for dietary iron. Poult. Sci. 48:1810. (Abstr.)

Hill, C. H., and G. Matrone. 1961. Studies on copper and iron deficiencies in growing chicks. J. Nutr. 73:425–431.

Kubena, L. F., J. D. May, J. W. Deaton, F. N. Reece, and B. D. Lott. 1972. Effect of dietary iron and copper on mortality of chicks at two temperatures. Poult. Sci. 51:1470–1471.

LINOLEIC ACID

Balnave, D. 1970. Essential fatty acids in poultry nutrition. World's Poult. Sci. J. 26:442–460.

Balnave, D., and S. T. C. Weatherup. 1974. The necessity of supplementing laying hen diets with linoleic acid. Br. Poult. Sci. 15:325-331.

Calvert, C. C. 1965. The performance of female Japanese quail on linoleic acid deficient diets. Poult. Sci. 44:1358. (Abstr.)

Ketola, H. G., R. J. Young, and M. C. Nesheim. 1973. Linoleic acid requirement of turkey poults. Poult. Sci. 52:597-603.

Menge, H. 1968. Linoleic requirement of the hen for reproduction. J. Nutr. 95:578-582.

Menge, H. 1970a. Comparative requirements of linoleic acid for male and female chicks. Poult. Sci. 49:178-183.

Menge, H. 1970b. Further studies on the linoleic acid requirement of the hen using purified and practical type diets. Poult. Sci. 49:1027-1030.

MAGNESIUM

Almquist, H. J. 1942. Magnesium requirement of the chick. Proc. Soc. Exp. Biol. Med. 49:544-545.

Bird, F. H. 1946. Magnesium supplementation in relation to a previously reported cerebellar disorder in chicks. Poult. Sci. 25:396-397.

Bird, F. H. 1949. Magnesium deficiency in the chick. I. Clinical and neuropathologic findings. J. Nutr. 39:13-30.

Edwards, H. M., Jr., and D. Nugara. 1968. Magnesium requirement of the laying hen. Poult. Sci. 47:963-966.

Gardner, E. E., J. C. Rogler, and H. E. Parker. 1960. Magnesium requirement of the chick. Poult. Sci. 39:1111-1115.

Hajj, R. N., and J. L. Sell. 1969. Magnesium requirement of the laying hen for reproduction. J. Nutr. 97:441-448.

Nugara, D., and H. M. Edwards, Jr. 1963. Influence of dietary Ca and P levels on the Mg requirement of the chick. J. Nutr. 80:181-184.

Sell, J. L., R. Hajj, A. Cox, and W. Guenter. 1967. Effect of magnesium deficiency in the hen on egg production and hatchability. Br. Poult. Sci. 8:55-60.

Sullivan, T. W. 1964. Studies on the dietary requirement and interaction of magnesium with antibiotics in turkeys to 4 weeks of age. Poult. Sci. 43:401-405.

Vohra, P. 1972. Magnesium requirement for survival and growth of Jananese quail (Coturnix coturnix japonica). Poult. Sci. 51:2103-2105.

MANGANESE

Cox, A. C., and S. L. Balloun. 1969. Manganese requirements of laying hens as related to diet calcium. Poult. Sci. 48:745-747.

Gallup, W. D., and L. C. Norris. 1939a. The amount of manganese required to prevent perosis in the chick. Poult. Sci. 18:76-82.

Gallup, W. D., and L. C. Norris. 1939b. The effect of a deficiency of manganese in the diet of the hen. Poult. Sci. 18:83-88.

Gutowska, M. S., and R. T. Parkhurst. 1942. Studies in mineral nutrition of laying hens. 1. The manganese requirement. Poult. Sci. 21:277-287.

Van Reen, R., and P. B. Pearson. 1955. Manganese deficiency in the duck. J. Nutr. 55:225-234.

Watson, L. T., C. B. Ammerman, S. M. Miller, and R. H. Harms. 1971. Biological availability to chicks of manganese from different inorganic sources. Poult. Sci. 50:1693-1700.

NIACIN

Adams, R. L., and C. W. Carrick. 1967. A study of the niacin requirement of the laying hen. Poult. Sci. 46:712-718.

Battig, M. J., E. G. Hill, T. H. Canfield, and H. J. Sloan. 1953. Prevention of perosis in goslings by nicotinic acid. Poult. Sci. 32:550-551.

Briggs, G. M., Jr., R. C. Mills, C. A. Elvehjem, and E. B. Hart. 1942. Nicotinic acid in chick nutrition. Proc. Soc. Exp. Biol. Med. 51:59-61.

Briggs, G. M., Jr., T. D. Luckey, L. J. Teply, C. A. Elvehjem, and E. B. Hart. 1943. Studies on nicotinic acid deficiency in the chick. J. Biol. Chem. 148:517-522.

Childs, G. R., C. W. Carrick, and S. M. Hauge. 1952. The niacin requirement of young chickens. Poult. Sci. 31:551-558.

Fisher, H., H. M. Scott, and B. C. Johnson. 1954. Quantitative aspects of the niacin-tryptophan relationship in the chick. Poult. Sci. 33:1054-1055. (Abstr.)

Gropp, J., V. Schulz, G. Sauerwein, and J. Tiews. 1972. The nicotinic acid activity of nicotinic acid nitrile and estimation of the niacine requirement of Japanese quail. Int. J. Vitam. Nutr. Res. 42:205-213.

Hartfiel, W., and I. Kirchner. 1973. Significance of nicotinic acid and its influence on the liver lipid content of the laying hen. Gefluegelkd. Arch. 73:114.

Hegsted, D. M. 1946. Nutritional studies with the duck. III. Niacin deficiency. J. Nutr. 32:467-472.

Jukes, T. H., E. L. R. Stokstad, and M. Belt. 1947. Deficiencies of certain vitamins as studied with turkey poults on a purified diet. J. Nutr. 33:1-12.

Patterson, E. B., J. R. Hunt, P. Vohra, L. G. Blaylock, and J. McGinnis. 1956. The niacin and tryptophan requirements of chicks. Poult. Sci. 35:499-504.

Ringrose, R. C., G. Athanasios, A. G. Manoukas, R. Hinkson, and A. E. Teeri. 1965. The niacin requirement of the hen. Poult. Sci. 44:1053-1056.

Scott, M. L. 1953. Prevention of the enlarged hock disorder in turkeys with niacin and vitamin E. Poult. Sci. 32:670-677.

Scott, M. L., and G. F. Heuser. 1952. Studies in duck nutrition. Poult. Sci. 31:752-754.

Scott, M. L., E. R. Holm, and R. E. Reynolds. 1959. Studies on the niacin, riboflavin, choline, manganese and zinc requirements of young ringnecked pheasants for growth, feathering, and prevention of leg disorders. Poult. Sci. 38:1344-1350.

Sunde, M. L. 1955. The niacin requirement of chickens from 6 to 11 weeks. Poult. Sci. 34:304-311.

Sunde, M. L., and H. R. Bird. 1957. The niacin requirement of the young ringneck pheasant. Poult. Sci. 36:34-42.

PANTOTHENIC ACID

Balloun, S. L., and R. E. Phillips. 1957. Interaction effects of vitamin B12 and pantothenic acid in breeder hen diets on hatchability, chick growth and livability. Poult. Sci. 36:929-934.

Bauernfeind, J. C., L. C. Norris, and G. F. Heuser. 1942. The pantothenic acid requirement of chicks. Poult. Sci. 21:142-146.

Beer, A. E., M. L. Scott, and M. C. Nesheim. 1963. The effects of graded levels of pantothenic acid on the breeding performance of White Leghorn pullets. Br. Poult. Sci. 4:243-253.

Fisher, H., and C. B. Hudson. 1956. Chick viability and pantothenic acid deficiency in the breeding diet—a case report. Poult. Sci. 35:487–488.

Fox, M. R. S., G. Q. Hudson, and M. E. Hintz. 1966. Pantothenic acid requirement of young Japanese quail. Fed. Proc. 25:721. (Abstr.)

Gillis, M. B., G. F. Heuser, and L. C. Norris. 1948. Pantothenic acid in the nutrition of the hen. J. Nutr. 35:351–363.

Hegsted, D. M., and R. L. Perry. 1948. Nutritional studies with the duck. J. Nutr. 35:411–417.

Kratzer, F. H., and D. Williams. 1948. The pantothenic acid requirement of poults for early growth. Poult. Sci. 27:518–523.

Kratzer, F. H., P. N. Davis, B. J. Marshall, and D. E. Williams. 1955. The pantothenic acid requirement of turkey hens. Poult. Sci. 34:68–72.

Scott, M. L., E. R. Holm, and R. E. Reynolds. 1964. Studies on the pantothenic acid and unidentified factor requirements of young ringnecked pheasants and Bobwhite quail. Poult. Sci. 43:1534–1539.

Serafin, J. A. 1974. Studies on the riboflavin, niacin, pantothenic acid and choline requirements of young Bobwhite quail. Poult. Sci. 53:1522–1532.

Waisman, H. A., R. C. Mills, and C. A. Elvehjem. 1942. Factors required by chicks maintained on a heated diet. J. Nutr. 24:187–198.

PHOSPHORUS (AND CALCIUM)

Davidson, J., and A. W. Boyne. 1970. The calcium and phosphorus requirements of laying hens. Br. Poult. Sci. 11:231–240.

Dean, W. F. 1972. Recent findings in duck nutrition. Proc. Cornell Nutr. Conf., pp. 77–85.

Gillis, M. B., L. C. Norris, and G. F. Heuser. 1949. The effect of phytin on the phosphorus requirement of the chick. Poult. Sci. 28:283–292.

Miller, M. W., and G. E. Bearse. 1934. Phophorus requirements of laying hens. Wash. State Univ. Agric. Exp. Stn. Tech. Bull. 306.

Nelson, F. E., J. K. Lauber, and L. Mirosh. 1964. Calcium and phosphorus requirement for the breeding Coturnix quail. Poult. Sci. 43:1346. (Abstr.)

O'Rourke, W. F., H. R. Bird, P. H. Phillips, and W. W. Cravens. 1954. The effect of low phosphorus rations on egg production and hatchability. Poult..Sci. 33:1117–1122.

Roland, D. A., Sr., and R. H. Harms. 1976. The influence of feeding diets containing different calcium-phosphorus ratios on the laying hen. Poult. Sci. 55:637–641.

Scott, M. L., A. Antillon, and L. Krook. 1976. Effects of calcium-phosphorus interrelationships upon egg shell quality. Proc. Cornell Nutr. Conf., pp. 122–126.

Singsen, E. P., L. D. Matterson, and H. M. Scott. 1947. Phosphorus in poultry nutrition. J. Nutr. 33:13–26.

Sullivan, T. W. 1959. Phosphorus requirement of turkeys for late growth. Poult. Sci. 38:1252. (Abstr.)

Summers, J. D., R. Grandhi, and S. Leison. 1976. Calcium and phosphorus requirements of the laying hen. Poult. Sci. 55:402–413.

Sunde, M. L., and H. R. Bird. 1956. A critical need of phosphorus for the young pheasant. Poult. Sci. 35:424–430.

Watkins, W. E., and H. H. Mitchell. 1930. The phosphorus requirements of growing chickens with a demonstration of the value of controlled experimental feeding. Poult. Sci. 15:32–41.

Wilson, H. R., M. W. Holland, Jr., and R. H. Harms. 1972. Dietary calcium and phosphorus requirements for Bobwhite chicks. J. Wildl. Manage. 36:965–968.

POTASSIUM

Ben-Dor, B. 1941. Requirement of potassium by the chick. Proc. Soc. Exp. Biol. Med. 46:341–343.

Gillis, M. B. 1948. Potassium requirement of the chick. J. Nutr. 36:351–357.

Leach, R. M. 1974. Studies on the potassium requirement of the laying hen. J. Nutr. 104:684–686.

Leach, R. M., Jr., R. Dam, T. R. Ziegler, and L. C. Norris. 1959. The effect of protein and energy on the potassium requirement of the chick. J. Nutr. 68:89–100.

Sullivan, T. W. 1963. Studies on the potassium requirement of turkeys to 4 weeks of age. Poult. Sci. 42:1072–1075.

PROTEIN

Allen, N. K., and R. J. Young. 1973. Amino acid and protein requirements of laying Japanese quail. Fed. Proc. 32:894. (Abstr.)

Andrews, T. L., R. H. Harms, and H. R. Wilson. 1973. Protein requirement of the Bobwhite chick. Poult. Sci. 52:2199–2201.

Baldini, J. T., R. E. Roberts, and C. M. Kirkpatrick. 1950. A study of the protein requirements of Bobwhite quail reared in confinement in battery brooders to eight weeks of age. Poult. Sci. 29:161–166.

Balloun, S. L., and G. M. Speers. 1969. Protein requirements of laying hens as affected by strain. Poult. Sci. 48:1175–1188.

Blair, R., and R. J. Young. 1974. Egg production responses of Coturnix quail to dietary additions of nitrogen in the form of amino acids, diammonium citrate and intact protein. Poult. Sci. 53:391–400.

Bragg, D. B., and A. I. Akinwande. 1973. The nutritional value of wheat protein for early growth of layer and broiler breeder pullets. Poult. Sci. 52:1646–1651.

Clandinin, D. R., and A. R. Robblee. 1958. Optimum calorie to protein ratio for pheasant starters. Poult. Sci. 37:1194. (Abstr.)

Couch, J. R., and J. K. Royton. 1974. Amino acids and protein in broiler nutrition. Poult. Sci. 53:750–755.

Cvetanov, I., R. Doncev, and S. Kumanov. 1969. Requirements for protein and energy in mixed feeds for laying ducks. Zivotnovadni Nauki 6:19–25.

Dean, W. F., M. L. Scott, and R. J. Young. 1965. Protein requirement of ducklings at different stages of growth. Poult. Sci. 44:1363. (Abstr.)

Heuser, G. F. 1941. Protein in poultry nutrition—a review. Poult. Sci. 20:362–368.

Hunt, J. R., and J. R. Aitken. 1970. Age and strain effects on protein requirements of layers. Poult. Sci. 49:1399. (Abstr.)

Lepore, P. D., and H. L. Marks. 1971. Growth rate inheritance in Japanese quail. 5. Protein and energy requirements of lines selected under different nutritional environments. Poult. Sci. 50:1335–1341.

March, B. E., and J. Biely. 1972. The effects of protein level and amino acid balance in wheat-based laying rations. Poult. Sci. 51:547–557.

Merritt, E. S., and J. R. Aitken. 1961. Raising geese. Canadian Department of Agriculture Publication No. 848.

Minear, L. R., D. L. Miller, and S. L. Balloun. 1972. Protein requirements of turkey breeder hens. Poult. Sci. 51:2040–2043.

Mussehl, F. E., C. W. Ackerson, and R. H. Thayer. 1941. Protein utilization by the growing poult. Poult. Sci. 20:469. (Abstr.)

Nivas, S. C., and M. L. Sunde. 1969. Protein requirements of layers per day and phase feeding. Poult. Sci. 48:1672–1678.

Norris, L. C., L. J. Elmore, R. C. Ringrose, and G. Bump. 1936. The protein requirement of ringnecked pheasant chicks. Poult. Sci. 15:454–459.

Roberson, R. H., and D. W. Francis. 1963a. The effect of protein level, iodinated casein and supplemental methionine on the performance of White Chinese geese. Poult. Sci. 42:863–867.

Roberson, R. H., and D. W. Francis. 1963b. The effect of energy and protein levels of the ration on the performance of White Chinese geese. Poult. Sci. 42:867–871.

Roberson, R. H., and D. W. Francis. 1963c. The effect of protein and energy levels of the ration on carcass characteristics of White Chinese geese. Poult. Sci. 42:872–875.

Roberts, R. E. 1940. Levels of protein in rations for young turkeys. Purdue Univ. Agric. Exp. Stn. Res. Bull. 448.

Scott, M. L., and G. F. Heuser. 1951. Studies in duck nutrition. Poult. Sci. 30:164–167.

Scott, M. L., G. F. Heuser, and L. C. Norris. 1948. Energy, protein, and unidentified vitamins in poult nutrition. Poult. Sci. 27:773–780.

Scott, M. L., E. R. Holm, and R. E. Reynolds. 1954. Studies on pheasant nutrition. Poult. Sci. 33:1237–1244.

Stockland, W. L., and L. G. Blaylock. 1974a. The influence of ration protein level on the performance of floor reared and cage reared replacement pullets. Poult. Sci. 53:790–800.

Stockland, W. L., and L. G. Blaylock. 1974b. The influence of temperature on the protein requirement of cage reared replacement pullets. Poult. Sci. 53:1174–1187.

Sunde, M. L. 1956. The energy and protein relationship for poultry. Proc. 7th Nutr. Sch. Feed Men Univ. Wis., pp. 67–70.

Tanaka, T., T. Yamane, and T. Nishikawa. 1966. Influence of dietary protein and energy level on laying Japanese quail. Jpn. J. Zootech. Sci. 37:231.

Thayer, R. H., G. E. Hubbell, J. A. Kasbohm, R. D. Morrison, and E. C. Nelson. 1974. Daily protein intake requirement of laying hens. Poult. Sci. 53:354–364.

Touchburn, S. P., and E. C. Naber. 1962. Effect of nutrient density and protein-energy interrelationships on reproductive performance of the hen. Poult. Sci. 41:1481–1488.

Twining, P. V., Jr., O. P. Thomas, E. H. Bossard, and J. L. Nicholson. 1974. The effect of amino acid and protein level on body composition of 8½ week broilers. Proc. Md. Nutr. Conf., pp. 89–95.

Vogt, H. 1966. The decrease of the protein content in the ration in the second growing period of Japanese quail. Dtsch. Geflugelwirtschaft. 18:174.

Vogt, H. 1967. Further experiments concerning the protein requirement of quail during the growing period. World's Poult. Sci. J. 23:263. From Arch. Geflugelkd. 31:211.

Vogt, H. 1969. Protein requirement of quail chicks in the early stages of rearing. Arch. Geflugelkd. 33:274–278.

Waibel, P. E. 1958. The feeding of geese and their potential in meat production. Feedstuffs, April 12, 1958.

Waibel, P. E. 1968. Amino acids and protein for growing turkeys. Minn. Nutr. Conf. Proc., p. 149.

Waibel, P. E. 1975. The challenge of meeting protein and amino acid needs of growing turkeys. Feedstuffs, January 6, 1975.

Weber, C. W., and B. L. Reid. 1967. Protein requirements of Coturnix quail to five weeks of age. Poult. Sci. 46:1190–1194.

PYRIDOXINE

Briggs, G. M., Jr., R. C. Mills, D. M. Hegsted, C. A. Elvehjem, and E. B. Hart. 1942. The vitamin B$_6$ requirement of the chick. Poult. Sci. 21:379–383.

Cravens, W. W., E. E. Sebesta, J. G. Halpin, and E. B. Hart. 1946. Studies on the pyridoxine requirements of laying and breeding hens. Poult. Sci. 25:80–82.

Daghir, N. J., and S. L. Balloun. 1963. Evaluation of the effect of breed on vitamin B$_6$ requirements of chicks. J. Nutr. 79:279–288.

Daghir, N. J., and M. A. Shah. 1973. Effect of dietary protein level on vitamin B$_6$ requirement of chicks. Poult. Sci. 52:1247.

Fuller, H. L., and W. S. Dunahoo. 1959. The effect of various drug additives on the vitamin B$_6$ requirement of chicks. Poult. Sci. 38:1150–1154.

Fuller, H. L., and P. E. Kifer. 1959. The vitamin B$_6$ requirement of chicks. Poult. Sci. 38:255–260.

Fuller, H. L., R. C. Field, R. Roncalli-Amici, W. S. Dunahoo, and H. M. Edwards. 1961. The vitamin B$_6$ requirement of breeder hens. Poult. Sci. 40:249–253.

Gries, C. L., and M. L. Scott. 1972. The pathology of pyridoxine deficiency in chicks. J. Nutr. 102:1259–1267.

Hegsted, D. M., and M. N. Rao. 1945. Nutritional studies with the duck. J. Nutr. 30:367–374.

Hogan, A. G., L. R. Richardson, H. Patrick, D. L. O'Dell, and H. L. Kempster. 1941. Vitamin B$_6$ and chick nutrition. Poult. Sci. 20:180–183.

Kirchgessner, M., and D. A. Maier. 1968. Estimation of the vitamin B$_6$ requirement of broilers. Arch. Geflugelkd. 32:415–419.

Kratzer, F. H., F. H. Bird, V. S. Asmundson, and S. Lepkovsky. 1947. The comparative pyridoxine requirement of chicks and turkey poults. Poult. Sci. 26:453–456.

Maier, D. A., and M. Kirchgessner. 1968. On the vitamin B$_6$ requirement of broilers. Arch. Geflugelkd. 32:415–419.

Sullivan, T. W., H. M. Heil, and M. E. Armintrout. 1967. Dietary thiamine and pyridoxine requirements of young turkeys. Poult. Sci. 46:1560–1564.

Waldroup, P. W., J. F. Maxey, L. W. Luther, B. D. Jones, and M. L. Nesheim. 1976. Factors affecting the response of turkeys to biotin and pyridoxine supplementation. Exp. Stn. Bull. 805, Univ. Ark., Fayetteville.

RIBOFLAVIN

Bethke, R. M., and P. R. Record. 1942. The relation of riboflavin to growth and curled-toe paralysis in chicks. Poult. Sci. 21:147–154.

Bolton, W. 1944. The riboflavin requirement of the White Wyandotte chick. J. Agric. Sci. 34:198–206.

Bolton, W. 1947. The riboflavin requirement of the White Wyandotte chick. J. Agric. Sci. 37:316–322.

Boucher, R. V., F. W. Hill, H. Patrick, and H. C. Knandel. 1941. The riboflavin requirement of turkeys for hatchability. Poult. Sci. 20:456. (Abstr.)

Boucher, R. V., H. Patrick, and H. C. Knandel. 1942. The riboflavin requirement of turkeys for hatchability and growth. Poult. Sci. 21:466. (Abstr.)

Davis, H. J., L. C. Norris, and G. F. Heuser. 1938. Further

evidence on the amount of vitamin G required for reproduction in poultry. Poult. Sci. 17:87-93.

Hegsted, D. M., and R. L. Perry. 1948. Nutritional studies with the duck. J. Nutr. 35:411-417.

Heuser, G. F., H. S. Wilgus, and L. C. Norris. 1938. The quantitative vitamin G requirement of chicks. Poult. Sci. 17:105-108.

Hill, F. W., L. C. Norris, and M. L. Scott. 1954. The riboflavin requirement of Single Comb White Leghorns for reproduction. Poult. Sci. 33:1059. (Abstr.)

Norris, L. C., H. S. Wilgus, Jr., A. T. Ringrose, V. Heiman, and G. F. Heuser. 1936. The vitamin G requirement of poultry. Cornell Univ. Agric. Exp. Stn. Bull. 660.

Patrick, H., M. I. Darrow, and C. L. Morgan. 1944. The role of riboflavin in turkey poult nutrition. Poult. Sci. 23:146-148.

Petersen, C. F., C. E. Lampman, and O. E. Stamberg. 1947a. Effect of riboflavin intake on egg production and riboflavin content of eggs. Poult. Sci. 26:180-186.

Petersen, C. F., C. E. Lampman, and O. E. Stamberg. 1947b. Effect of riboflavin on hatchability of eggs from battery confined hens. Poult. Sci. 26:187-191.

Scott, M. L., E. R. Holm, and R. E. Reynolds. 1959. Studies on the niacin, riboflavin, choline, manganese and zinc requirements of young ringnecked pheasants for growth, feathering, and prevention of leg disorders. Poult. Sci. 38:1344-1350.

Serafin, J. A. 1974. Studies on the riboflavin, niacin, pantothenic acid and choline requirements of young Bobwhite quail. Poult. Sci. 53:1522-1532.

Waibel, P. E., and T. H. Canfield. 1957. Studies on riboflavin needs of goslings. Unpublished data.

Wyatt, R. D., H. T. Tung, W. E. Donaldson, and P. B. Hamilton. 1973. A new description of riboflavin deficiency syndrome in chickens. Poult. Sci. 52:237-244.

SELENIUM

Gries, C. L., and M. L. Scott. 1972. Pathology of selenium deficiency in the chick. J. Nutr. 102:1287-1296.

Moxon, A. L. 1937. Alkali disease or selenium poisoning. S. D. Agric. Exp. Stn. Bull. 311.

National Research Council, Committee on Animal Nutrition, Subcommittee on Selenium. 1971. Selenium in Nutrition. National Academy of Sciences, Washington, D.C.

Poley, W. E., and A. L. Moxon. 1938. Tolerance levels of seleniferous grains in laying rations. Poult. Sci. 17:72-76.

Scott, M. L. 1966. Studies on the interrelationship of selenium, vitamin E and sulfur amino acids in a nutritional myopathy of the chick. Ann. N.Y. Acad. Sci. 138:82-89.

Scott, M. L., G. Olson, L. Krook, and W. R. Brown. 1967. Selenium-responsive myopathies of myocardium and of smooth muscle in the young poult. J. Nutr. 91:573-583.

Thompson, J. N., and M. L. Scott. 1968. Selenium deficiency in chicks and its effect on the requirement for vitamin E. Fed. Proc. 27:417. (Abstr.)

Thompson, J. N., and M. L. Scott. 1969. Role of selenium in the nutrition of the chick. J. Nutr. 97:335-342.

Thompson, J. N., and M. L. Scott. 1970. Impaired lipid and vitamin E absorption related to atrophy of the pancreas in selenium-deficient chicks. J. Nutr. 100:797-809.

Tully, W. C., and K. W. Franke. 1935. A new toxicant occurring naturally in certain samples of plant foodstuffs. VI. A study of the effect of affected grains on growing chicks. Poult. Sci. 14:280-284.

Walter, E. D., and L. S. Jensen. 1963. Effectiveness of selenium and non-effectiveness of sulfur amino acids in preventing muscular dystrophy in the turkey poult. J. Nutr. 80:327-331.

SODIUM AND CHLORINE

Burns, C. H., W. W. Cravens, and P. H. Phillips. 1953. The sodium and potassium requirements of the chick and their interrelationship. J. Nutr. 50:317-329.

Dean, W. F. 1972. Recent findings in duck nutrition. Proc. Cornell Nutr. Conf., pp. 77-85.

Kumpost, H. E., and T. W. Sullivan. 1966. Minimum sodium requirement and interaction of potassium and sodium in the diet of young turkeys. Poult. Sci. 45:1334-1339.

Leach, R. M., Jr., and M. C. Nesheim. 1963. Studies on chloride deficiency in chicks. J. Nutr. 81:193-199.

McWard, G. W., and H. M. Scott. 1961. Sodium requirement of the young chick fed purified diets. Poult. Sci. 40:1026-1029.

Nesheim, M. C., R. M. Leach, Jr., T. R. Zeigler, and J. A. Serafin. 1964. Interrelationships between dietary levels of sodium, chlorine and potassium. J. Nutr. 84:361-366.

Scott, M. L., A. van Teinhoven, E. R. Holm, and M. E. Reynolds. 1960. Studies on the sodium, chlorine, and iodine requirements of young pheasants and quail. J. Nutr. 71:282-288.

THIAMINE

Arnold, A., and C. A. Elvehjem. 1938. Studies on the vitamin B_1 requirement of growing chicks. J. Nutr. 15:403-410.

Gries, C. L., and M. L. Scott. 1972. The pathology of thiamin, riboflavin, pantothenic acid and niacin deficiencies in the chick. J. Nutr. 102:1269-1285.

Polin, D., W. H. Ott, E. R. Wynosky, and C. C. Porter. 1963. Estimation of thiamine requirement for optimum hatchability from the relationship between dietary and yolk levels of the vitamin. Poult. Sci. 42:925-928.

Robenalt, R. C. 1960. The thiamine requirement of young turkey poults. Poult. Sci. 39:354-360.

Thornton, P. A. 1960. Thiamine requirement of growing chicks as influenced by breed differences. Poult. Sci. 39:440-444.

Thornton, P. A., and J. V. Shutze. 1960. The influence of dietary energy level, energy source, and breed on the thiamine requirement of chicks. Poult. Sci. 39:192-199.

TOXICITY: INORGANIC ELEMENTS

Adams, A. W., A. J. Kahrs, and J. L. West. 1967. Effect of sodium nitrate in the drinking water on performance of turkeys. Poult. Sci. 46:1226. (Abstr.)

Arrington, L. R., R. A. Santa Cruz, R. H. Harms, and H. R. Wilson. 1967. Effects of excess dietary iodine upon pullets and laying hens. J. Nutr. 92:325-330.

Arthur, D., I. Motzok, and H. D. Branion. 1958. Interaction of dietary copper and molybdenum in rations fed to poultry. Poult. Sci. 37:1181. (Abstr.)

Berg, L. R. 1963. Evidence of vanadium toxicity resulting from the use of certain commercial phosphorus supplements in chick rations. Poult. Sci. 42:766-769.

Berg, L. R. 1965. Effect of diet composition on vanadium toxicity for the chick. Poult. Sci. 44:1351. (Abstr.)

Berg, L. R., and R. D. Martinson. 1972. Effect of diet composition on the toxicity of zinc for the chick. Poult. Sci. 51:1690-1695.

Berg, L., G. E. Bearse, and L. H. Merrill. 1963. Vanadium toxicity in laying hens. Poult. Sci. 42:1407-1411.

Carlson, C. W., and F. Leitis. 1957. Methionine, betaine, and choline as counteractants of selenium toxicity. Poult. Sci. 36:1108. (Abstr.)

Chicco, C. F., C. B. Ammerman, P. A. Van Walleghem, P. W.

Waldroup, and R. H. Harms. 1967. Effects of varying dietary ratios of magnesium, calcium, and phosphorus in growing chicks. Poult. Sci. 46:368–373.

Damron, B. L., C. F. Simpson, and R. H. Harms. 1969. The effects of feeding various levels of lead on the performance of broilers. Poult. Sci. 48:1507–1509.

Davies, R. E., B. L. Reid, A. A. Kurnick, and J. R. Couch. 1960. The effect of sulfate on molybdenum toxicity in the chick. J. Nutr. 70:193–198.

Deobold, H. J., and C. A. Elvehjem. 1935. The effect of feeding high amounts of soluble iron and aluminum salts. Am. J. Physiol. 111:118–123.

Doberenz, A. R., A. A. Kurnick, B. J. Hulett, and B. L. Reid. 1965. Bromide and fluoride toxicities in the chick. Poult. Sci. 44:1500–1504.

Gardiner, E. E., H. E. Parker, and C. W. Carrick. 1959. Soft phosphate in chick rations. Poult. Sci. 38:721–727.

Harper, J. A., and G. H. Arscott. 1962. Salt as a stress factor in relation to pendulous crop and aortic rupture in turkeys. Poult. Sci. 41:497–499.

Hathcock, J. N., C. H. Hill, and G. Matrone. 1964. Vanadium toxicity and distribution in chicks and rats. J. Nutr. 82:106–110.

Hill, C. H. 1974. Influence of high levels of minerals on the susceptibility of chicks to *Salmonella gallinarum*. J. Nutr. 104:1221–1226.

Hill, C. H., G. Matrone, W. L. Payne, and C. W. Barber. 1963. *In vivo* interactions of cadmium with copper, zinc, and iron. J. Nutr. 80:227–235.

Hill, C. H., B. Starcher, and G. Matrone. 1964. Mercury and silver interrelationships with copper. J. Nutr. 83:107–110.

Jensen, L. S. 1975a. Precipitation of a selenium deficiency by high dietary levels of copper and zinc. Proc. Soc. Exp. Biol. Med. 149:113–116.

Jensen, L. S. 1975b. Modification of a selenium toxicity in chicks by dietary silver and copper. J. Nutr. 105:769–775.

Jensen, L. S., R. P. Peterson, and L. Falen. 1974. Inducement of enlarged hearts and muscular dystrophy in turkey poults with dietary silver. Poult. Sci. 53:57–64.

Johnson, D., Jr., A. L. Mehring, Jr., F. X. Savins, and H. W. Titus. 1962. The tolerance of growing chickens for dietary zinc. Poult. Sci. 41:311–317.

Krista, L. M., C. W. Carlson, and O. E. Olson. 1961. Some effects of saline waters on chicks, laying hens, poults and ducklings. Poult. Sci. 40:938–944.

Kunishisa, Y., T. Yaname, T. Tanaka, I. Fukuda, and T. Nishikava. 1966. The effect of dietary chromium on the performance of chicks. Jpn. Poult. Sci. 3:10–14.

Lepore, P. D., and R. F. Miller. 1965. Embryonic viability as influenced by excess molybdenum in chicken breeder diets. Proc. Soc. Exp. Biol. Med. 118:155–157.

Mayo, R. H., S. M. Hauge, H. E. Porter, F. N. Andrews, and C. W. Carrick. 1956. Copper tolerance of young chickens. Poult. Sci. 35:1156. (Abstr.)

Mehring, A. L., Jr., J. H. Brumbaugh, A. J. Sutherland, and H. W. Titus. 1960. The tolerance of growing chickens for dietary copper. Poult. Sci. 39:713–719.

Moxon, A. L., and W. O. Wilson. 1944. Selenium-arsenic antagonism in poultry. Poult. Sci. 23:149–151.

Mugler, D. J., J. D. Mitchell, and A. W. Adams. 1970. Factors affecting turkey meat color. Poult. Sci. 49:1510–1513.

Nesheim, M. C., R. M. Leach, Jr., T. R. Zeigler, and J. A. Serafin. 1964. Interrelationships between dietary levels of sodium, chlorine, and potassium. J. Nutr. 84:361–366.

Nugara, D., and H. M. Edwards, Jr. 1963. Influence of dietary Ca and P levels on the Mg requirement of the chick. J. Nutr. 80:181–184.

Parkhurst, C. R., and P. Thaxton. 1973. Toxicity of mercury in young chicks. 1. Effect on growth and mortality. Poult. Sci. 52:273–276.

Peterson, R. P., and L. S. Jensen. 1975a. Induced exudative diathesis in chicks by dietary silver. Poult. Sci. 54:795–798.

Peterson, R. P., and L. S. Jensen. 1975b. Interrelationships of dietary silver with copper in the chick. Poult. Sci. 54:771–775.

Poupoulis, C., and L. S. Jensen. 1976. Effect of high dietary copper on gizzard integrity of the chick. Poult. Sci. 55:113–121.

Roberson, R. H., and P. J. Schaible. 1960. The tolerance of growing chicks for high levels of different forms of zinc. Poult. Sci. 39:893–896.

Roberts, R. E. 1957. Salt tolerance of turkeys. Poult. Sci. 36:672–673.

Romoser, G. L., W. A. Dudley, L. J. Machlin, and L. Loveless. 1961. Toxicity of vanadium and chromium for the growing chick. Poult. Sci. 40:1171–1173.

Sell, J. L., and W. K. Roberts. 1963. Effects of dietary nitrate on the chick: growth, liver vitamin A stores and thyroid weight. J. Nutr. 79:171–178.

Storer, N. L., and T. S. Nelson. 1968. The effect of various aluminum compounds on chick performance. Poult. Sci. 47:244–247.

Sunde, M. L. 1964. The use of the turkey poult as a test animal for nitrite toxicity. Poult. Sci. 43:1368. (Abstr.)

Supplee, W. C. 1961. Production of zinc deficiency in turkey poults by dietary cadmium. Poult. Sci. 40:827–828.

Supplee, W. C. 1964. Observations on the effect of copper additions to purified turkey diets. Poult. Sci. 43:1599–1600.

Taucins, E., A. Svilane, A. Valdmanis, A. Buike, R. Zarina, and E. Fedorova. 1969. Fiziol. Akt. Komponenty Pitan. Zhivotn, pp. 199–212.

Turk, J. L., Jr., and F. H. Kratzer. 1960. The effects of cobalt in the diet of the chick. Poult. Sci. 39:1302. (Abstr.)

Vohra, P., and F. H. Kratzer. 1968. Zinc, copper and manganese toxicities in turkey poults and their alleviation by EDTA. Poult. Sci. 47:699–704.

Waibel, P. E., D. C. Snetsinger, R. A. Ball, and J. H. Sautter. 1964. Variation in tolerance of turkeys to dietary copper. Poult. Sci. 43:504–506.

Weber, C. W., and B. L. Reid. 1968. Nickel toxicity in growing chicks. J. Nutr. 95:612–616.

Weber, C. W., and B. L. Reid. 1971. Cadmium studies in chicks. Poult. Sci. 50:1644. (Abstr.)

Weber, C. W., A. R. Doberenz, R. W. G. Wyckoff, and B. L. Reid. 1968. Strontium metabolism in chicks. Poult. Sci. 47:1318–1323.

Weber, C. W., A. R. Doberenz, and B. L. Reid. 1969. Fluoride toxicity in the chick. Poult. Sci. 48:230–235.

TRACE ELEMENTS

Carlisle, E. M. 1972. Silicon—an essential element for the chick. Fed. Proc. 31:700. (Abstr.)

Carlisle, E. M. 1974. Essentiality and function of silicon, pp. 407–424. *In* W. G. Hoekstra, J. W. Suttie, H. E. Ganther, and W. Mertz, ed., Trace Element Metabolism in Animals, vol. 2. University Park Press, Baltimore, Md.

Hopkins, L. L., Jr. 1974. Essentiality and function of vanadium, pp. 397–406. *In* W. G. Hoekstra, J. W. Suttie, H. E. Ganther, and W. Mertz, ed., Trace Element Metabolism in Animals, vol. 2. University Park Press, Baltimore, Md.

Leach, R. M., and L. C. Norris. 1957. Studies on factors affecting the response of chicks to molybdenum. Poult. Sci. 36:1136. (Abstr.)

Nielsen, F. H. 1974. Essentiality and function of nickel, pp. 381–385. In W. G. Hoekstra, J. W. Suttie, H. E. Ganther, and W. Mertz, ed., Trace Element Metabolism in Animals, vol. 2. University Park Press, Baltimore, Md.

Nielsen, F. H., and D. A. Ollerich. 1973. Studies on a vanadium deficiency in chicks. Fed. Proc. 32:929.

Nielsen, F. H., and D. A. Ollerich. 1974. Nickel: a new essential trace element. Fed. Proc. 33:1767–1772.

Reid, B. L., A. A. Kurnick, R. N. Burroughs, R. L. Svacha, and J. R. Couch. 1957. Molybdenum in poult nutrition. Proc. Soc. Exp. Biol. Med. 94:737–740.

Schwarz, K. 1974. New essential trace elements (SU, V, F, Si): progress report and outlook, pp. 355–380. In W. G. Hoekstra, J. W. Suttie, H. E. Ganther, and W. Mertz, ed., Trace Element Metabolism in Animals, vol. 2. University Park Press, Baltimore, Md.

Schwarz, K. 1974. Recent dietary trace element research exemplified by tin, fluorine and silicon. Fed. Proc. 33:1748–1757.

UNIDENTIFIED NUTRIENTS

Arscott, G. H., and G. F. Combs. 1955. Unidentified growth factors required by chicks and poults. Poult. Sci. 34:843–850.

Berg, L. R., and W. W. Lawrence. 1971. Cottonseed meal, dehydrated grass and ascorbic acid as dietary factors preventing toxicity of vanadium for the chick. Poult. Sci. 50:1399–1404.

Blair, R., M. L. Scott, and R. J. Young. 1972. Unidentified factor activities in whole soybeans required for optimum growth of Coturnix quail. J. Nutr. 102:1529–1541.

Chang, C. H., and P. E. Waibel. 1970. Efficacy of zinc bacitracin and sources of unidentified growth factors with corn-soybean meal type diet for turkey poults. Poult. Sci. 49:733–743.

Chang, C. H., L. Falen, and L. S. Jensen. 1974. Effect of maternal diet on the response of Japanese quail to purified and practical diets. Poult. Sci. 53:265–272.

Creger, C. R., M. E. Hague, and J. R. Couch. 1961. Reproduction studies in the mature fowl. 1. Corn and soybean oil meal as sources of unidentified growth and hatchability factors. Poult. Sci. 40:299–302.

Dixon, T., and J. R. Couch. 1970. Distillers dried solubles as a source of unidentified growth factors required by the chick and poult. Poult. Sci. 49:392–401.

Harrison, G. F., and M. E. Coates. 1964. Studies of the growth promoting activity for chicks of fish solubles. Br. J. Nutr. 18:461–466.

Jensen, L. S., and C. H. Chang. 1976. Fractionation studies on a factor in linseed meal protecting against selenosis in chicks. Poult. Sci. 55:594–599.

Mason, M. E., J. Sacks, and E. L. Stephenson. 1961. Isolation and nature of an unidentified growth factor in condensed fish solubles. J. Nutr. 75:253–264.

Sunde, M. L., W. W. Cravens, C. A. Elvehjem, and J. G. Halpin. 1950. An unidentified factor required by chicks fed practical rations. Poult. Sci. 29:204–207.

Touchburn, S. P., R. D. M. Silva, and E. C. Naber. 1974. Further evidence for an unidentified nutrient in fish solubles which improves hatchability and progeny growth of turkeys and Japanese quail. Poult. Sci. 53:1745–1758.

Waldroup, P. W., and H. O. Rutherford. 1971. Acceptability of corn dried steep liquor concentrate for laying hens and turkeys. Poult. Sci. 50:1863–1867.

VITAMIN A

Almquist, H. J. 1953. Evaluation of vitamin requirement data. Poult. Sci. 32:122–128.

Almquist, H. J., and E. Mecchi. 1939. Vitamin A requirements of laying hens. Poult. Sci. 18:129–137.

Bearse, G. E., and M. W. Miller. 1937a. The vitamin A requirements of White Leghorn pullets during the growing period. Poult. Sci. 16:34–38.

Bearse, G. E., and M. W. Miller. 1937b. The effect of varying levels of vitamin A in the hen ration on the vitamin A content of the egg yolk, on hatchability and on chick livability. Poult. Sci. 16:39–43.

Berger, H., and G. Gebhardt. 1969. Relations between vitamin A and protein supplies of growing ducks. 4. Effect of different amounts of protein on the requirement for vitamin A. Jahrb. Tierenahrung Futterung 7:399–409.

Biely, J., and W. Chalmers. 1936. Vitamin A requirements of growing chicks. Can. J. Res. Sec. D 14:21–24.

Chavez, R., C. R. Creger, and J. R. Couch. 1963. Vitamin A requirements of growing turkeys. Poult. Sci. 42:1259–1260. (Abstr.)

Coles, B., J. Biely, and B. E. March. 1970. Vitamin A deficiency and Eimeria acervulina infection in the chick. Poult. Sci. 49:1295–1301.

Couch, J. R., C. R. Creger, and R. Chavez. 1971. The vitamin A requirement for growing turkeys. Br. Poult. Sci. 12:367–371.

Frohring, W. O., and J. Wyeno. 1934. Carotene and vitamin A requirements for White Leghorn chicks. J. Nutr. 8:463–479.

Guilbert, H. R., and W. R. Hinshaw. 1934. Vitamin A storage in the livers of turkeys and chickens. J. Nutr. 8:45–56.

Hill, F. W., M. L. Scott, L. C. Norris, and G. F. Heuser. 1961. Reinvestigation of the vitamin A requirements of laying and breeding hens and their progeny. Poult. Sci. 40:1245–1254.

Hinshaw, W. R., and W. E. Lloyd. 1934. Vitamin A deficiency in turkeys. Hilgardia 8:281–304.

Jensen, L. S. 1965. Vitamin A requirement of breeding turkeys. Poult. Sci. 44:1609–1610.

Jungherr, E. 1943. Nasal histopathology and liver storage in subtotal vitamin A deficiency of chickens. Univ. Conn. Agric. Exp. Stn. Bull. 250.

Marusich, W., and J. C. Bauernfeind. 1963. The biological activity of beta-carotene in poultry and rats. Poult. Sci. 42:949–957.

McClary, C. F., G. E. Bearse, and V. L. Miller. 1939. Vitamin A requirements of laying hens. West. Wash. Agric. Exp. Stn. Annu. Rep., pp. 45–46.

Nestler, R. B. 1946. Vitamin A, vital factor in the survival of bobwhites. Trans. 11th N. A. Wildl. Conf., pp. 176–195.

Olsen, E. M., J. D. Harvey, D. C. Hill, and H. D. Branion. 1959. Effect of dietary protein and energy levels on the utilization of vitamin A and carotene. Poult. Sci. 38:942–949.

Parrish, D. B., R. A. Zimmerman, P. E. Sanford, and E. Hung. 1963. Utilization of alfalfa carotene and vitamin A by growing chicks. J. Nutr. 79:9–17.

Record, P. R., R. M. Bethke, and O. H. M. Wilder. 1935. Vitamin A requirements of growing chicks. Poult. Sci. 14:297. (Abstr.)

Record, P. R., R. M. Bethke, and O. H. M. Wilder. 1937. The vitamin A requirement of chicks, with observations on the comparative efficiency of carotene and vitamin A. Poult. Sci. 16:25–33.

Ringrose, R. C., and L. C. Norris. 1936. A study of the vitamin A requirement of the chick during early life. Poult. Sci. 15:390–396.

Rubin, M., and H. R. Bird. 1942. Relation of vitamin A to egg production and hatchability. Md. Univ. Agric. Exp. Stn. Tech. Bull. A12.

Rubin, M., H. R. Bird, and H. M. DeVolt. 1941. Avitaminosis A in commercial poultry flocks. Poult. Sci. 20:155–160.

Rusoff, L. L., and N. R. Mehrhof. 1939. Shark liver oil—a potent source of vitamin A for poultry. Poult. Sci. 18:339–344.

Russell, W. C., C. S. Platt, M. W. Taylor, and D. F. Chichester. 1936. The vitamin A requirement of the laying pullet. N. J. Agric. Exp. Stn. Circ. 369.

Sherwood, R. M., and G. S. Fraps. 1932. Quantities of vitamin A required by pullets for maintenance and egg production. Tex. Agric. Exp. Stn. Bull. 468.

Sherwood, R. M., and G. S. Fraps. 1934. The amount of vitamin A potency required by hens for egg production. Tex. Agric. Exp. Stn. Bull. 493.

Sherwood, R. M., and G. S. Fraps. 1935. The vitamin A requirements of hens for egg production. Tex. Agric. Exp. Stn. Bull. 514.

Sherwood, R. M., and G. S. Fraps. 1940. Requirements of chickens for vitamin A when fed as carotene. Tex. Agric. Exp. Stn. Bull. 583.

Stoewsand, G. S., and M. L. Scott. 1961. The vitamin A requirements of breeding turkeys and their progeny. Poult. Sci. 40:1255–1262.

Taylor, M. W., and W. C. Russell. 1947. The provitamin A requirement of growing chickens. Poult. Sci. 26:234–242.

Taylor, M. W., J. R. Stern, and W. C. Russell. 1947. The provitamin A requirement of hens. Poult. Sci. 26:243–254.

Tepper, A. E., and R. C. Durgin. 1938. Vitamin A requirements of growing chicks. N.H. Univ. Agric. Exp. Stn. Bull. 310.

Thornton, P. A., and W. A. Whittet. 1962. The influence of dietary energy level, energy source, breed, and sex on vitamin A requirement in the chick. Poult. Sci. 41:32–36.

Williams, J. K., C. E. Lampman, and D. W. Bolin. 1939. The efficiency of carotene as supplied by alfalfa meal in meeting the vitamin A requirements of laying hens. Poult. Sci. 18:268–275.

Wilson, W. O., C. H. Schroeder, and W. A. Higgins. 1936. Further studies on the vitamin A requirements of chicks. Poult. Sci. 15:426. (Abstr.)

VITAMIN B₁₂

Baldini, J. T., R. E. Roberts, and C. M. Kirkpatrick. 1953. Antibiotic and vitamin B₁₂ supplements as related to crude protein level of Bobwhite quail diets. Poult. Sci. 32:563–567.

Chin, D., J. B. Anderson, R. F. Miller, L. C. Norris, and G. F. Heuser. 1958. The vitamin B₁₂ requirement of White Leghorn hens. Poult. Sci. 37:335–343.

Davis, R. L., and G. M. Briggs. 1951. The vitamin B₁₂ requirement of the chick. Poult. Sci. 30:628–629.

Fox, M. R. S., L. O. Ortiz, and G. M. Briggs. 1956. Effect of dietary fat on requirement of vitamin B₁₂ by the chick. Proc. Soc. Exp. Biol. Med. 93:501–504.

Johnson, E. L. 1954. Vitamin B₁₂ requirements of hens as affected by choline and penicillin. Poult. Sci. 33:100–107.

Johnson, E. L. 1955. Turkeys require vitamin B₁₂ and choline. Poult. Sci. 34:1013–1016.

Looi, S. H., and R. Renner. 1974. Effect of feeding "carbohydrate-free" diets on the chicks' requirement for vitamin B₁₂. J. Nutr. 104:394–399.

Mariakulandai, A., and J. McGinnis. 1952. The vitamin B₁₂ requirement for hatchability of chicken eggs. Poult. Sci. 32:3–7.

Miller, R. F., L. C. Norris, and G. F. Heuser. 1956. The vitamin B₁₂ requirement of White Leghorn chicks. Poult. Sci. 35:342–349.

Ott, W. H. 1951. Further studies of the activity of crystalline vitamin B₁₂ for chick growth. Poult. Sci. 30:86–91.

Ott, W. H., E. L. Rickes, and T. R. Wood. 1948. Activity of crystalline vitamin B₁₂ for chick growth. J. Biol. Chem. 174:1047–1048.

Petersen, C. F., A. C. Wiese, R. V. Dahlstrom, and C. E. Lampman. 1952. Influence of vitamin B₁₂ and antibiotics on hatchability. Poult. Sci. 31:129–132.

Petersen, C. F., A. C. Wiese, G. E. Milne, and C. E. Lampman. 1953. Vitamin B₁₂ requirements for hatchability and production of high-quality chicks. Poult. Sci. 32:535–542.

Rys, R., and J. Koreleski. 1974. The effect of dietary propionic acid on the requirement of chicks for vitamin B₁₂. Br. J. Nutr. 31:143–146.

Sherwood, D. H., and H. J. Sloan. 1954. Vitamin B₁₂ and choline in corn-soy rations for starting poults. Poult. Sci. 33:1015–1021.

Stokstad, E. L. R., T. H. Jukes, J. Pierce, A. C. Page, Jr., and A. L. Franklin. 1949. The multiple nature of the animal protein factor. J. Biol. Chem. 180:647–654.

Wiese, A. C., C. F. Petersen, R. V. Dahlstrom, and C. E. Lampman. 1952. Effect of vitamin B₁₂ intake of hens upon carry-over in chicks. Poult. Sci. 31:851–854.

VITAMIN D

Association of Official Agricultural Chemists. 1955. Official and Tentative Methods of Analysis, 8th ed. AOAC, Washington, D.C.

Baird, F. D., and D. J. Greene. 1935. The comparative vitamin D requirements of growing chicks, turkeys, and pheasants. Poult. Sci. 14:70–82.

Biely, J., and B. E. March. 1967. Calcium and vitamin D in broiler rations. Poult. Sci. 46:223–232.

Bird, H. R. 1944. Comparison of response of turkey poults and of chicks to different forms of vitamin D. J. Nutr. 27:377–383.

Black, D. J. G., and M. E. Coates. 1948. The vitamin D requirements of intensively kept ducklings. VIIIth World's Poult. Congr. 1:96–102.

Boucher, R. V. 1944. Efficacy of vitamin D from different sources for turkeys. J. Nutr. 27:403–413.

Bragg, D. B., J. Floyd, and E. L. Stephenson. 1971. Factors affecting the transfer of Ca⁴⁵ from the hens' diet to the eggshell. Poult. Sci. 50:167–173.

Fritz, J. C., W. Archer, and D. Barker. 1941. Vitamin D requirements of ducklings. Poult. Sci. 20:151–154.

Fritz, J. C., J. H. Hooper, and H. P. Moore. 1945. Calcification in the poult. Poult. Sci. 24:324–328.

Garlich, J. D., and R. D. Wyatt. 1971. Effects of increased vitamin D₃ on calcium retention and eggshell calcification. Poult. Sci. 50:950–956.

Hammond, J. C. 1941. The vitamin D requirement of turkey poults. Poult. Sci. 20:204–205.

McGinnis, J., and R. J. Evans. 1946. Response of turkey poults to vitamin D from different sources. Poult. Sci. 25:521–525.

Motzok, I., and H. D. Branion. 1946. The vitamin D requirements of growing ducks. Poult. Sci. 27:482–485.

Murphy, R. R., J. E. Hunter, and H. C. Knandel. 1936. The vitamin D requirements of growing chicks and laying hens. Pa. State Univ. Agric. Exp. Stn. Bull. 334.

Scott, M. L., E. R. Holm, and R. E. Reynolds. 1958. The calcium, phosphorus, and vitamin D requirements of young pheasants. Poult. Sci. 37:1419–1425.

Shue, G. M. 1967. Vitamin D requirements of young Japanese quail. Fed. Proc. 26:697. (Abstr.)

Singsen, E. P., L. D. Matterson, and H. M. Scott. 1947. Phosphorus in poultry nutrition. III. The relationship between the source of vitamin D and the utilization of cereal phosphorus by the poult. J. Nutr. 33:13–26.

Stadelman, W. J., R. V. Boucher, and E. W. Callenbach. 1950. The effect of vitamin D in the turkey breeder ration on egg production and hatchability and on growth and calcification of the poults. Poult. Sci. 29:146–152.

Waldroup, P. W., C. B. Ammerman, and R. H. Harms. 1963. The relation of phosphorus, calcium, and vitamin D₃ in the diet of broiler-type chicks. Poult. Sci. 42:982–989.

Waldroup, P. W., J. E. Stearns, C. B. Ammerman, and R. H. Harms. 1965. Studies on the vitamin D₃ requirement of the broiler chick. Poult. Sci. 44:543–548.

Wilhelm, L. A., E. I. Robertson, and M. Rhian. 1941. The effect of the level of vitamin D on egg production and hatchability of Bronze turkey hens. Poult. Sci. 20:565–569.

Yang, H. S., P. E. Waibel, and J. Brenes. 1973. Evaluation of vitamin D₃ supplements by biological assay using the turkey. J. Nutr. 103:1187–1194.

VITAMIN E

Atkinson, R. L., T. M. Ferguson, J. H. Quisenberry, and J. R. Couch. 1955. Vitamin E and reproduction in turkeys. J. Nutr. 55:387–397.

Bartov, I., and S. Bornstein. 1972. Nutritional factors affecting the occurrence of experimental encephalomalacia in chicks. Poult. Sci. 51:868–876.

Bartov, I., T. Budowski, and S. Bornstein. 1965. The relation between alpha-tocopherol content of the breeder diet and that of the newly hatched chick. Poult. Sci. 44:1489–1494.

Combs, G. F., and M. L. Scott. 1974. Dietary requirements for vitamin E and selenium measured at the cellular level in the chick. J. Nutr. 104:1292–1296.

Ferguson, T. M., R. L. Atkinson, and J. R. Couch. 1954. Relationship of vitamin E to embryonic development of avian eye. Proc. Soc. Exp. Biol. Med. 86:868–871.

Jensen, L. S. 1968. Vitamin E and essential fatty acids in avian reproduction. Fed. Proc. 27:914–919.

Jensen, L. S., and J. McGinnis. 1957. Studies on the vitamin E requirement of turkeys for reproduction. Poult. Sci. 36:1344–1350.

Jensen, L. S., M. L. Scott, G. F. Heuser, L. C. Norris, and T. S. Nelson. 1956. Studies on the nutrition of breeding turkeys. Poult. Sci. 35:810–816.

Machlin, J. L., and G. S. Gordon. 1962. Etiology of exudative diathesis, encephalomalacia, and muscular degeneration in the chicken. Poult. Sci. 41:473–477.

Scott, M. L. 1962. Antioxidants, selenium, and sulfur amino acids in the vitamin E nutrition of chicks. Nutr. Abstr. Rev. 32:1 8.

Scott, M. L., M. C. Nesheim, and R. J. Young. 1969. Nutrition of the Chicken. M. L. Scott and Associates, Publishers, Ithaca, N.Y.

Tengerdy, R. T., and C. F. Nockels. 1973. The effect of vitamin E on egg production, hatchability and humoral immune response of chickens. Poult. Sci. 52:778–783.

VITAMIN K

Charles, O. W., and T. M. Huston. 1972. The biological activity of vitamin K materials following storage and pelleting. Poult. Sci. 51:1421–1427.

Dean, W. F. 1972. Recent findings in duck nutrition. Proc. Cornell Nutr. Conf., pp. 77–85.

Griminger, P. 1957. On the vitamin K requirement of turkey poults. Poult. Sci. 36:1227–1235.

Nelson, T. S., and L. C. Norris. 1960. Studies on the vitamin K requirement of the chick. J. Nutr. 72:137–144.

Nelson, T. S., and L. C. Norris. 1961a. Studies on the vitamin K requirement of the chick. Poult. Sci. 40:392–395.

Nelson, T. S., and L. C. Norris. 1961b. Studies on the vitamin K requirement of the chick. J. Nutr. 73:135–142.

WATER

Adams, A. W. 1973. Consequences of depriving laying hens of water a short time. Poult. Sci. 52:1221–1223.

Enos, H. L., R. E. Morenz, and W. A. Whittet. 1967. Shade materials, growth and water consumption of turkeys. Poult. Sci. 46:1412–1421.

Haller, R. W., and M. L. Sunde. 1966. The effects of withholding water on the body temperature of poults. Poult. Sci. 45:991–997.

Kellerup, S. U., J. W. Parker, and G. H. Arscott. 1965. Effect of restricted water consumption on broiler chickens. Poult. Sci. 44:78–83.

Medway, W., and M. R. Kare. 1959. Water metabolism of the growing domestic fowl with special reference to water balance. Poult. Sci. 38:631–637.

Parker, J. T., M. A. Boone, and J. F. Knechtges. 1972. The effect of ambient temperature upon body temperature, feed consumption and water consumption using two varieties of turkeys. Poult. Sci. 51:659–664.

Wilson, W. O., E. H. McNally, and H. Ota. 1957. Temperature and calorimeter study on hens in individual cages. Poult. Sci. 36:1254–1261.

XANTHOPHYLL

Bartov, I., and S. Bornstein. 1974. Carotenoids in poultry production symposium. Proc. XV World's Poult. Congr., pp. 245–246.

Couch, J. R., A. A. Camp, and F. M. Farr. 1971. The supplementary effect of adding canthaxanthin to a diet containing natural sources of pigmenting compounds on the pigmentation of broilers. Br. Poult. Sci. 12:205–211.

Couch, J. R., and F. M. Farr. 1971. Evaluation of beta-apo 8' caratenal. Br. Poult. Sci. 12:87–93.

Fritz, J. C. 1962. Feeding for egg yolk color. Feedstuffs 34(19):44–48.

Fry, J. L., and R. H. Harms. 1975. Yolk color, candled egg grade and xanthophyll availability from dietary natural pigmenting ingredients. Poult. Sci. 54:1094–1101.

Madiedo, G., and M. L. Sunde. 1964. The effect of algae, dried lake weed, alfalfa and ethoxyquin on yolk color. Poult. Sci. 44:1056–1061.

Sunde, M. L. 1962. The effect of different levels of vitamin A, beta-apo 8' caratenal and alfalfa on yolk color. Poult. Sci. 41:532–541.

Milton Keynes UK
Ingram Content Group UK Ltd.
UKHW021256090824
1218UKWH00009B/88